To Lou,
    Best wishes + happy cooking
                    Jim Haller

The Blue Strawbery Cookbook

The

COOKING
(BRILLIANTLY)
WITHOUT
RECIPES

THE HARVARD COMMON PRESS

Blue Strawbery Cookbook

by James Haller

The Harvard Common Press
The Common, Harvard, Massachusetts 01451

Printed in the United States of America

Library of Congress Cataloging in Publication Data

Haller, James.
     The Blue Strawbery Cookbook.

     Includes index.
     1. Cookery.   I. Title.
TX652.H34   641.5   76-23990
ISBN 0-916782-06-9 (hardcover)
ISBN 0-916782-05-0 (paperback)

Cover illustration by George Stavrinos
Text illustrations by Martha Dillard

2   3   4   5   6   7   8   9   10

For
Mark John Burke
who discovered a blue strawbery one golden afternoon
and has since
faithfully and lovingly tended the vine;
and Gene Brown
whose genius turned a lot of secondhand chairs and dishes
into a most successful Broadway opening on Ceres Street;
and Albert Boulanger
without whom I'd never have had the freedom
to be a cuckoo cookoo.

Thank you gentlemen
for the best Karma I've ever had.

Acknowledgments

My most grateful appreciation to Walter and Judy Jackson who have continued to say yes; Burton Trafton, Jr. and Mervyn Bronson, who also said yes; Donald and Ruby Perkins, who made starting all over a very pleasant time; the New Hampshire Liquor Commission under the direction of Costas Tentas and, locally, George Mouflouze; the Holts of Portsmouth Navigation; Michael Shears for all those wonderful dishes; to our neighbors those first years — Jerry and Bea Van Horn, Barbara and Hodgdon, Al Corbin and Tom — who were courteous to our customers when they walked into their apartments by mistake; and to Marguerite Mathews, who never got fat tasting my soups or keeping my Karma; to Michael McGinley, Jamie Locke, Greg Dodge, Roger Richards, Bruce Downing, Ray McCracken, Bernie Tato, Eddie Wydra, Donna Stafford, Alan Hamm, Terry Kidder, and Steve Brown; to Bob Wiggins and the crowd at Portsmouth Produce, who continue to send me the best vegetables in the country; to Babe Marcono of the Blue Fin Fish Market, who taught me a lot about fish; to Evelyn Hobson, a dear friend and newspaperwoman who gave us, in Foster's Daily Democrat, our very first review; to Annette Hall, who the first time she saw me one wintry Sunday afternoon gave me a piece of lapis lazuli that looked like a strawbery; to Dick Morton, whose generosity will always be remembered; and to the beautiful city of Portsmouth, New Hampshire. And to my grandma, Agnes Kostecki Guy, who taught me to sing while I cook.

Preface

To understand the value of this cookbook one has to understand something about James Haller, his personality, character, and ideas. One has to understand, as well, the unique group consisting of James Haller, Gene Brown, Mark Burke, and Albert Boulanger.

It was six years ago that I met James Haller for the first time, while visiting the Blue Strawbery on the recommendation of some friends of mine. The dinner I had that evening is hard to describe, since the Blue Strawbery is like and unlike other restaurants. It serves a fixed-menu dinner, in a room tastefully furnished and decorated with a keen eye for elegance and detail. It doesn't seat more than thirty-six people. What is unlike other small restaurants being created in this time of renaissance of gourmet cooking is the food and the lack of a menu card. Few of the courses are named, but each is described in great detail when served. This is as true for the salad dressing as it is for the delicious pheasant with chocolate based sauce. The reason for this is the simple fact that every course is a creation in itself. During my visits to the Blue Strawbery I have never had two courses which tasted completely the same. There is always a new detail in the aroma and the fragrance of the dish which makes it unique and different from any other time it was created before.

As I said before, one has to learn to know James Haller to understand his approach to cooking. It is really an approach to life that is basically existential. I have learned to know James Haller and his close associates over the years; I am interested in gourmet cooking as the dean of a college which has a hotel program, and I am generally interested in people as a social psychologist. Haller is a creative person; his mind and actions can bring seemingly impossible opposites toward elegant combinations. His mind is always wandering toward the new. His eyes see the beauty of details, and his taste recognizes what is different. Most of all, however, James Haller likes to share his impressions and creations with others. He is, in this respect, the original artist that Joyce Cary describes: "He loves and serves the beauty that exists . . . and either accepts that beauty, that formal construction of feeling and ideas, as matter of course, and takes off from it into new invention, or he reacts violently against it."

James Haller reacts violently against everything that is prescriptive and of the ordinary. But above all, he is an educator in the true sense of the word. He doesn't teach what is right and wrong; he helps the people around him to discover the new. He has transmitted this characteristic not only to his close friends but to anyone who comes into contact with him and his work. One of the most creative things that one can do, in my opinion, is to write a cookbook without recipes—it is then that one has to teach people courage and trust in themselves. James Haller encourages people to listen to their own rhythms and creativity, which he believes are within everyone. It is one thing to be creative. It is another thing, however, to believe deeply and to let the world know that every person has his or her unique qualities, to be imaginatively employed in the creation of our daily bread.

Jan E. Clee, Dean
The Whittemore School
University of New Hampshire
September, 1976

Contents

Introduction

There is really only one secret for cooking brilliantly without recipes: Never follow the rules! The moment you begin to follow a rule you are hampered by restrictions and if you are restricted you cannot create. Because everyone has to eat, the art of cooking should be an effortless joy for everyone.

Food is the first and most important of the necessities of life, and simply because it is basic it should be utterly fantastic. In the present economy it's the basic commodities that have become the most expensive and, at the same time, the poorest quality, both in concept and material. The same situation is evident in the decline and fall of all the past great civilizations. That's something to think about the next time you eat a Twinkie.

I am convinced that the lack of honesty in our society stems from two generations of unconcerned and untalented parents and schools who bought and prepared every single "convenience" food on the market. The advertising media succeeded in convincing them that convenience foods are timesaving, money-saving, and sexy. No one is concentrating on quality, just on the "effect." Convenience foods are an effect. You add a cup of boiling water to an envelope of chemicals and — *poof!* — you have the effect of a cup of soup. Compare that with your other necessities of life.

The best way to change all that is to start with what you eat, since eating is the function over which you have the most control. We truly are what we eat; it might not manifest itself by turning us into Fig Newtons, but it can cause our values and attitudes and appreciations to be sterile, uninspired, and often completely false. Your existence should be like a festive banquet, even to the nuts and fruitcakes.

NUTRITION

If it's fresh it's nutritious. I am always amazed when I eat food prepared by "nutritional experts" — the people who actually go to school to learn how to prepare the kind of food you get in hospitals, schools, and institutions. If you've ever eaten at any of those places you must know what I'm talking about. I recently had occasion to spend one night in the hospital. For a hundred and sixty dollars I was rudely awakened from a deep and healing sleep and offered a breakfast of instant cereal made with powdered milk, a small pot of instant coffee, and two slices of white toast made from that styrofoam they pass off as bread. The night before I had been given a dinner of canned creamed corn, and an ancient and badly prepared prestuffed and frozen green pepper. I simply did not eat it for fear of my health.

The fact that the government supports teaching nutritionists to open cans of creamed corn should lead you to the conclusion that the government doesn't know beans about nutrition. Purely from a metaphysical viewpoint, how nutritious can a food be if you don't enjoy it? And, at a more practical level, how nutritious is a food if you don't eat it? If an educational system supports that kind of training of "cooks," it stands to reason the same kind of education will produce our other "authorities"—lawyers, doctors, teachers, clergy, law officers, and politicians. The prospect is truly frightening.

Cynicism is the worst of all possible appetizers; but I say all this because this is what cooking is to me. It is good to understand the concept of cooking from as many different places as possible, so that nothing in the kitchen—or anywhere else—is ever an unpleasant surprise, but rather a joyful discovery.

Nutrition—anything fresh! The incredible vegetables that exist! Artichokes and asparagus and kohlrabi, Belgian endive, hearts of palm, parsnips, rutabagas, collard greens, and watercress. They can be soups and sauces and sherbets and salads and accompaniments. They can become souffles and custards and quiches and often desserts. Consider, if you will, a sweet potato and Amaretto ripple ice cream, a collard green vichyssoise, mushrooms and chestnuts in chocolate brandy and sour cream. Begin an intake of romantic reality; one day the outcome will be profound.

If it's fresh it's nutritious. If it's canned or packaged or frozen or pre-prepared or dehydrated or imitation and contains chemicals then it is simply not very nutritious, no matter what the FDA or Madison Avenue tells us. You need only thaw an ice cube and drink it to understand what happens to all food that's been frozen. Have you ever asked a waitress if something on the menu was fresh and have her reply that it was "fresh frozen"? I completely understand that the peas or corn in question might have been taken off the vine, rushed in from the fields, and plunged into a temperature of eight thousand degrees below zero, but what, pray tell, exactly does that mean when six months later it's thawing out in a foot of hot, salty water?

The human body is a living, breathing organism. It is not logical to fill it with chemicals; we get enough of that in the air we breathe and the water we drink. You wouldn't fill a fifteen thousand dollar Jaguar with bulk oil and an inferior grade of gasoline, so why do less than the best for your own body, the most precise machine in creation?

COOKING UTENSILS

If it doesn't leak cook in it. The ridiculous myth of "proper utensils" is not only untrue, intimidating, and snobbish but also extremely expensive. Put the money into the food. Spending forty-five dollars for a copper saucepan trimmed with brass with a matching lid and filling it with a can of Ann Page Mexicorn is an action that speaks for itself. I am still using saucepans at Blue Strawbery that I bought in 1970 for a dollar and twenty-nine cents, and they are still perfectly functional. The fact that they cost a dollar twenty-nine hasn't affected the food in the least. If you want to make a quiche do it in a sixty-nine cent pie tin. If you feel as though you must have a souffle bake it in any deep dish that's ovenproof. Put the money into the food!

The very best cooking utensils I have ever found are the old cast-iron pots and pans. For about fifty dollars you can own different-sized frying pans, pots, muffin tins, stew pots, and roasters that will last all your life, as well as the lives of your children and probably your grandchildren. Aside from that you can go to any secondhand store and for ten dollars neatly furnish any kitchen with all the equipment necessary. Put the money into the food!

I also own a blender and an electric mixer, and find them both to be invaluable because of what they can help you achieve in the least amount of time. Good cooking should not be a thing that takes hours of effort.

It's nice to have a couple of cookie sheets and at least one cake pan, a very large pot for making soups and boiling lobsters, and a roasting pan with a cover for roasting turkeys and hams and legs of veal and lamb. It's also pleasant to have a couple of medium-sized saucepans for cooking vegetables and making sauces and, of course, fudge. And one nice-sized frying pan (with a cover) for frying chicken and pork chops and rabbit. However, if you don't want to invest that much time or money, or perhaps don't have the space for that many pots and pans, you can be completely equipped with just a frying pan, a fork, and a wooden spoon. Almost all the feats of good cooking—including an upside-down cake—can be performed in a frying pan.

SPICES

Spices and herbs are to cooking as color is to art. But even if all you ever used was salt, pepper, and sugar, the food would never become dull or uninspired: the number of flavorings that are available in the wonderful variety of fruits and vegetables is almost infinite. I often use fruits and vegetables for flavoring instead of a spice or herb; cutting an orange or lime or lemon into a pan of rice (not only for a unique flavor but because the citrus oils help to keep the rice fluffy and separated), or "spicing" asparagus, broccoli, string beans and the like with citrus juices and fruits, or cooking or saucing meats with berries and fruits and vegetables, and flavoring fruits with other fruits. Remember that any combination of foods can work depending on how you treat it, and often the only thing any combination needs to become an astonishing success is the simple addition of salt, pepper, or sugar.

Of course, it is a great luxury to own as many spices and herbs as are available. The best way to try out a spice or herb that is new to you is to whip it into mashed potatoes: they are the perfect vehicle because their own taste is bland enough, but has all the substance to adapt. If you buy those small bottles of spices you'll find suggestions for their uses on the back of the label. It's best not to pay any attention to these. Instead, use your spices on anything you like. Sprinkle dill on a grapefruit, caraway into mashed potatoes, curry on carrots. Be liberal with flavoring and one day you'll work up enough courage to fix swordfish in coffee brandy and sour cream and tarragon.

It's also good to remember that sweet is sweet. Rather than just using white sugar consider that brown sugar, molasses, sorghum, jams and jellies and preserves, honey, and maple sugar and syrup are also "sweets" and can be used as flavorings. Try parsnips baked in oranges and curry and honey, or acorn squash roasted in plum jam and apricot brandy, or sweet potatoes in nectarines and maple syrup.

By the same token, salty is salty. There are bouillons, soy sauce, tamari, vegetable extracts, and sea salts. As with sweets, by using different kinds of salts you can give your cooking a depth of taste that will immediately institute change. It takes only a small amount of courage to substitute a bouillon for salt, and the use of soy sauce or tamari does not necessarily mean you are making chop suey.

CUISINES—THEIRS, OURS, AND YOURS

It is undeniable that Europe has been the most artistic contributor to the world of cooking over the last several hundred years. European cuisine is incredible—in taste, presentation, style, and development. But though ethnic cooking of all kinds is always a joy to eat, for some people (mind you, I said "some") it is simply impossible to stick to a recipe. And to do a particular cuisine, you limit yourself to the options within that cuisine. If you don't, it will not be "theirs."

I find it inhibiting and often intimidating to follow a recipe; it stifles the creativity I like to feel while I cook. Following a recipe is somewhat like painting by number. You can be subtle, overbearing and heavy-handed, terrific or awful. But you can never improve upon the recipe. It has only become a "recipe" because someone else has perfected it.

One must continually grow, in or out of the kitchen, and if perfection implies limitation, where then does one have the opportunity to grow? Growth is found in discovery, and for me it has always been far more exciting to discover rather than perfect. In the six years I have been cooking at Blue Strawbery I doubt that I have ever created the same exact taste twice. It is not important to me. An artist would never paint exactly the same painting twice or three times; not only would it be dull, but the audience would quickly become bored. Imagine strolling through the Metropolitan Museum and seeing painting after painting exactly alike! The same principle applies to planning meals: "Oh look, here are the mashed potatoes with salt and pepper again... oh, and here are the Brussels sprouts boiled in salted water again...and tomorrow is Saturday, we'll have the hot dogs and pork and beans like we have every Saturday." The gallery would be the same if you were talking about a quiche, a Kiev, a lasagna, or a chow mein.

Inside all of us I believe there to be a field of pure creative intelligence. For the majority of people this field waits dormant and untouched because it is more convenient to follow a recipe, whether that recipe deals with a dinner, an ethic, or a political belief. Whenever we use a convenience rather than our imagination we do relinquish some part of our freedom, whether the convenience is a frozen dinner, or church every Sunday, or a liberation group, or a cynical attitude. Beginning simply to be free in the kitchen gives you a sense of worth that has immediate results and depends on no one other than you. If you can begin to inject this kind of liberation into other areas of your life you will indeed be cooking.

American cuisine—"ours"—can be New England, Southern, Midwestern, Southwestern, and the like; it is not so demanding in the preciseness of ingredients. Though Southern fried chicken is always dipped in batter, it could be a dozen different kinds of batter. New England fish chowder depends on subtlety and understatement—often difficult for the rest of the country to comprehend or practice.

That of course leaves "yours" in the world of cooking. Unbounded by recipes or tradition, its style is unique because it is yours. It is whatever *you* want it to be all of the time. It is not only what you have in the kitchen but what you don't have—like mixing soy sauce, lime juice, and onions into breadcrumbs to arrive at the taste of Parmesan cheese. It is free and completely creative, and because you are reaching for discovery rather than perfection it is continually exciting.

Within each of the chapters in this book I will give you guidelines for arriving at some of the dishes I have come up with at Blue Strawbery. The more unlikely-sounding the combinations, the better the opportunity; the more poetic the associations, the more romantic the outcome. The most important thing to remember is that any and every combination you can conceive of will work. Often the only thing you need to pull it all together is the simple addition of salt.

I never try out a recipe before I do it at Blue Strawbery. I walk into the kitchen knowing what I want the dish to look like and taste like; from there, it's just a matter of working backwards logically. I will try to show you the methods I use to make sure that I can be totally fearless in putting together new tastes.

The premise of this book is cooking without recipes. Once you arrive at an extraordinary success, you can always repeat it. But because it is your creation to begin with, you can feel confident that nothing should stop you from cooking it another way entirely.

NOTES ON EATING AND APPRECIATING

I am convinced that one of the reasons my grandmother was a spectacular cook was my grandfather. He always verbalized his appreciation of her cooking. One of the greatest inspirations any of us can have is to be appreciated, and that is something that just isn't taught anymore. Often people appreciate and even love what's being done for them but somehow do not know how to voice that enjoyment.

Children cannot grow to appreciate unless they are taught. They certainly don't get it in school, people rarely hear it at work, and those at home are almost never told how terrific their work's results are. It can only be discouraging to spend time cooking dinner and then to have everyone sit down, only to gobble it up and leave in ten minutes. Dinner should be the one time in the day when the entire family sits together for an hour or so to talk and enjoy a lovely, healthful, and personally prepared meal. It can be a form of communion, a time of civilization.

WHAT FOOD IS

A final word about food before I begin talking about food. Americans are so used to having everything packaged for them that it is often difficult to deal with the reality of whatever something is. In Europe if you go into a butcher shop you will see an entire animal hanging by its heels—rabbit, goat, squirrel, boar, and the like. Europeans see this from the time they are children, and from the time they are children they completely accept the concept of animals as edibles. But Americans are limited eaters. Beyond the usual beef, lamb, pork, chicken, and fish, carrots, potatoes, beans, and peas, there is an entire world of food that they completely ignore. In this country if you can find rabbit at all it is cut apart, skinned, cleaned, and frozen in a tiny box so that it looks very much like chicken. This is because the only time Americans think of rabbit is at Easter, and no one is keen on eating the Easter Bunny. The thought of squirrel or possum appalls the average sensibilities; and kidneys, brains, tripe, pigs' feet, tongue, and often liver are thought of as foreign or stigmatized by color, race, or religion—an absurd and bigoted concept. Americans are also hesitant to try squid, snails, octopus, eel, or almost anything that doesn't eventually look like a frozen fishstick. Though I am loath to hype the sale of anything from an economic standpoint, an amazing amount of money could be saved on a weekly food bill merely by being adventurous. Stews, chowders, spaghetti sauces, casseroles, sauces, and soups, entrees and appetizers, and whole dinners using uncommon foods can be inexpensive, healthful, delicious, and beautifully prepared. If your gastronomical courage must be fortified with a motivation other than adventure, economics is a terrific place to begin.

Soups

The principle of soup making is based, like all cooking, on simple logic. You need a pot large enough for the amount of soup you want to make, liquid and filling. The liquid may take any form: water, wine, juices, milk, cream, stock—anything that pours. The filling can be vegetables, fish, or meat; one specific ingredient, or a combination of several. The soup will need a salt to give it base—bouillon, salty cheeses, soy sauce, and tamari are all possibilities. While not essential, bones in a soup stock give it an added dimension.

THE CREAM SOUP

Butter, leeks, and cream are the basis of any great cream soup. To that concoction it is possible to add any vegetable in the world —squash, asparagus, peas, onions, sweet potatoes, collard greens, and cabbage are just a few. For liquid, use white wine— or sherry, or rose, or even red—or a juice, or a salty stock.

The leeks may also be shallots or white onions; you may leave them out altogether, but their addition gives an uncommon depth to soups that should not be missed. Both leeks and shallots are members of the onion family; the shallot looks a great deal like garlic, but it is not nearly so strong and is excellent for just about anything you wish to add it to.

I use potato for a thickening agent, but this may also be interchanged with other thickeners. If you use flour, add it at the very beginning so it will pick up the taste of the soup—nothing is more disappointing than a floury-tasting soup. Whipping egg yolks into the hot soup just before you serve it will also thicken the mixture. Almost any pulpy vegetable—parsnip, carrot, potato, turnip, squash—may be used for thickening. And enough of any vegetable blended into a puree will serve as well, though in that case it's always good to add a spoon or two of flour or a couple of well-beaten egg yolks for "binding." (Binding keeps the ingredients from separating. If your soup does separate after you've blended it, simply blend it again, or whip it with a whisk, eggbeater, or fork.)

Spice your cream soup with whatever your imagination can conjure up—not only the usual green herbs and spices, but chocolate, ginger, saffron, orange concentrate, flavored brandies and liqueurs...anything you happen to have handy. Cooks differ on the time to add the seasoning: some think you should add it in the beginning, others feel you should wait for the last fifteen minutes. The best idea is to add it whenever you please.

After learning the basics, all you really have to do is put it all into the pot and cook it. For instance, if you were to attempt a Broccoli and White Wine Cream Soup—loosely referred to as Broccoli Vichyssoise—for about six people it would be this simple:

Broccoli Vichyssoise   Into a pot large enough to hold soup for the amount of people you are cooking for melt a stick of butter; chop in a couple of washed leeks, one average-sized peeled potato, and the bushy part of a head of broccoli; add a glass of dry white wine, some white pepper, salt, and any spice of your choosing, and about a quart of light cream. Simmer it all until the potato is soft, and run it through a blender. You can serve it now, or you can place it in the freezer until it begins to freeze around the edges, whip it one more time, and serve ice cold.

(Broccoli Vichyssoise)

The magic—the brilliance—comes in the understanding of what goes with what; and that, of course, is always determined by your own particular taste. Don't be afraid of that: your taste is there to be recognized and opened up to. We are so conditioned by the "how to" and "what should" schools that we never experiment; and it's in experimentation that the most exciting discoveries occur.

For instance:

Suppose you fried a couple of peeled sweet potatoes in about half a stick of butter with one or two sliced leeks until they all became limp. Put them into a blender, add a glass of dry white wine, and blend until it becomes smooth. Put it back into the pot, add cream or milk, a handful of chopped chives, a comfortable amount of salt, some white pepper, some curry, and a shot of chocolate brandy. Then add a couple of handfuls of sliced fresh mushrooms and simmer the mixture, stirring often so that it doesn't become separated. When you feel the mushrooms are cooked, ladle the soup into serving-sized baking bowls, top each with a slice of Swiss, Muenster, cheddar, or mozzarella cheese, and bake it in a moderate oven until the cheese begins to crust. Serve piping hot. If you like, add a dab of sour cream on the top as you serve the soup. As soon as

Curried Chocolate Brandy and Mushroom Sweet Potato Cream Soup

you announce it is a "Curried Chocolate Brandy and Mushroom Sweet Potato Cream Soup," your audience will be so intrigued—or intimidated—that the rest of the meal is bound to be a success.

Soup is like a well dressed lady. The cream is the woman, the leeks her shoes, the butter her stockings, the wine her petticoat, the main ingredient her dress, and the spices her perfume. Using this analogy, remember that overdressing is cheap, understatement alluring because it offers mystery.

Corn and Pumpkin Chowder

In a soup pot melt one stick of butter until it sizzles. Add four or five washed and chopped leeks, about half a cup of flour for thickening, the kernels of six to eight ears of fresh corn, two cups of cooked pumpkin, a quart of light cream, half a bottle of chablis, one cup of dry sherry, two tablespoons of chicken base, a dash of white pepper to taste, a dash of allspice, and a quarter of a cup of sugar. While the mixture is cooking, fry a half pound of bacon until it is crisp. Drain and chip the bacon into tiny bits and add them to the chowder. Whip one blender full of the mixture until smooth. Then pour it into the pan you fried the bacon in and simmer to pick up the bacon flavor. Return this mixture to the soup pot and let it simmer for about half an hour. Pour the chowder into individual baking dishes, cover with a slice of Muenster cheese, and bake in a 400° oven for twenty to thirty minutes, or until the cheese becomes toasted on the top of the soup. Serve bubbling hot. Serves six to eight.

Since both corn and pumpkin are indigenous to the United States, nothing could be more American than Corn and Pumpkin Chowder.

FISH SOUPS

Keeping the pieces of fish intact and not lost in the confusion of other ingredients is the challenge of making a good fish soup. I like to make the broth first; when it's boiling hot, I pour it over the fish and serve. Fish should be cooked very little; the closer it is to raw the more subtle its flavors. Sometimes it is enough simply to heat the fish before serving.

There is an easy basic formula for fish stocks. At the fish market get a "rack"—the head, bones, and tail of the fish, left over after it has been filleted—and proceed as follows:

Basic Fish Stock

Place the rack in a soup pot and cover it with water. Add some dry sherry or white wine (or a little rose or even some red wine), a few onions, some herbs and spices such as saffron and rosemary, a couple of sliced tomatoes, and a spoon of peppercorns. Cover tightly and boil for about half an hour. Strain it out; add salt and pepper to taste and the juice from one lemon. Pour the strained stock, while it's boiling, over the bite-sized pieces of fish; let sit a few minutes, covered; and serve.

If you are making a cream fish soup, you might follow the same principle. Use milk in the soup pot instead of water, and add a pint of cream to the finished product. Thicken it with whatever agent you fancy, and blend it smooth before you pour it over the fish. Once again, feel free to add anything you like— shallots or leeks, a fine-chopped carrot or potato, chopped lettuce, or a combination of ingredients.

Creating a shellfish cream soup stock is almost too simple.

Shellfish Cream Soup

Instead of steaming or boiling your shellfish in water, simmer them in white wine for a few minutes, usually until they turn pink or red. Peel or

(Shellfish Cream Soup)

shell the crustacean, then place the shells back in the pot with the liquid. (If it's a lobster or crab, try to break the shells into as small pieces as possible.) Add a couple of cups of milk and boil the mixture while you are cutting apart the shellfish for the soup —it takes only a few minutes to boil a stock out of shells. Then strain the liquid, and add to the pot some butter, a little flour for thickening, salt, white pepper, and perhaps some tarragon. Slowly add the stock back into the flour and butter paste, stirring often so the mixture becomes creamy. Then add the shellfish, and about a pint of heavy cream. Salt and pepper to taste and let cook for fifteen to twenty minutes. You might also add a little dry sherry, some lemon or lime juice, a couple of sliced shallots, a few diced potatoes, or whatever you have an urge for. If it's too thick, add more white wine, cream, or milk; if it's too thin, make a flour and milk paste and stir it slowly back into the pot.

Baked Fruit-of-the-Sea Stew

Cut into small pieces about a quarter of a pound of salt pork and let it brown in the bottom of a soup pot. Drain off the grease, and add a half a stick of butter, two tablespoons of flour, a handful of thin-sliced shallots, a couple of bay leaves, a few sprinkles of curry, a good tablespoon of moist chicken base, salt and black pepper, and a small can of tomato paste. When this mixture begins to brown, add a chopped leek. Put it in a blender and puree it. This will make the base for the soup. Return it to the pot and add an onion sliced very thin, two cups of Clamato juice, half a cup of dry sherry, half a cup of white vermouth, half a cup of white wine and half a cup of dry red wine, the juice of one lemon, two chopped tomatoes, and a tablespoon of gumbo file (pulverized dried sassafras leaves). Simmer for forty-five minutes to an hour, then add a pint of raw oysters (with their juice), a cup of crabmeat, a cup of chopped uncooked and peeled shrimp, and half a pound of chopped squid. Simmer another fifteen minutes. Then fill the bottoms of individual baking dishes with bite-sized pieces of raw codfish, ladle the stew mixture over the cod, and bake in a 400° oven for about ten minutes. Serve bubbling.

(Fruit-of-the-Sea Stew)

SOME MORE GOOD SOUPS

I once heard a young stewardess ask an older friend, "How d'ya make a good pea soup?" The recipe that followed sounded like something you might be unfortunate enough to encounter while, in fact, riding that very airplane! I'd like to show you how to make a wonderful pea soup.

To begin with, you'll need a ham bone — the bigger the better, and with a little bit of ham left on it. Plunge it into an enormous pot of water, enough so that the bone is submerged, and turn on the heat for about six hours. About the second hour along, open a bag of dried peas and throw them in; let them boil and boil until they are finally soft. Then throw in a couple of diced carrots, a couple of chopped onions, a chopped celery stalk, a cup or two of dry white wine, maybe a potato chopped up or some leftover pieces of ham, a grab of sweet basil and a little sage, enough salt and black pepper to suit you — that is it. Don't fool around with bacon or sliced hot dogs or soaking the peas overnight. Takes all the fun out of it.

Pea Soup

Pretty much the same rule applies to any meat stock soup starting with bones. You simply fill the pot with water, boil the bones until you get a flavor, then add fresh vegetables, a couple of spices, a little base or salt and pepper, and a touch of wine or sherry.

Any liquid, even water—which I abhor using for cooking—will serve as a base for a soup. Hot cider for fruit soups, vegetable juices for meat or bouillon soups, or a squeeze of citrus juice in any soup—fruit, vegetable, meat, or fish—always enhances the basic substance of any concoction.

Here are some of the soups I have made at Blue Strawbery. I don't intend these instructions to be recipes, but instead hope that they will suggest inspired discoveries of your own.

Collard Green Cream Soup

Cover the bottom of your soup pot with about a quarter inch of melted butter; then wash and slice thin a couple of medium-sized leeks and simmer them in the butter until they become limp. Slice in one large peeled potato, and add two tablespoons of moist beef base, some salt and white pepper, and a glass of dry white wine or a bottle of beer. Cook on a low flame until the potatoes are soft. Then chop in one bunch of washed collards and fill the rest of the pot with light cream. Bring to a boil, stirring often so the cream doesn't stick to the bottom of the pot, and let it all simmer for about an hour. Put it into a blender and blend till smooth, add a handful of chives, and serve.

Collard Green Cream Soup may also be served chilled, in which case it should be called Collard Green Vichyssoise. And it makes a wonderful sauce for fresh salmon, hot or cold.

Cover the bottom of your soup pot with about a quarter inch of melted butter, slice in a couple of washed leeks and let them saute, and add a handful of flour for thickening, a couple of tablespoons of moist chicken base, some white pepper, two cloves of fresh garlic, a handful of chopped chives, and about half a cup of white vermouth. Then squeeze in the juice of one lime and add a couple of dashes of nutmeg. Slice six to eight tomatoes into the pot (cutting out the stems), and add enough milk or cream to completely cover the entire mixture. Let it simmer for about forty-five minutes, then run it all through the blender until it's smooth and pour it back into the pot. Add more cream if it's too thick, more tomatoes if it's too thin, and salt and white pepper to taste. Serve. This soup may also be served chilled.

Tomato and White Vermouth Cream Soup

Brown two washed and sliced leeks in a melted stick of butter. Add a handful of flour for thickening, a couple of tablespoons of moist beef base, about six medium (or twelve small) chopped white onions, white pepper to taste, a couple of dashes each of marjoram and thyme, and, if you have it, a good pinch of saffron. Stir the simmering mixture well, slowly adding a glass of dry white wine and a quart of light cream. Cook the soup until the onions are limp (half an hour to forty-five minutes), then ladle it into baking bowls and lay slices of cheese across the top. (Any cheese will do—Muenster, Swiss, cheddar, or mozzarella—as long as it doesn't come with each slice individually wrapped in plastic. Did you ever shake one of those pieces of cheese, holding it by the corner? It's like some kind of rubber.) Put the bowls of soup in a 400° oven for fifteen or twenty

Baked White Onion Cream Soup

minutes, and serve when the cheese is crusty and bubbling. Very nice served for lunch with a bowl of crisp romaine leaves and a little bottle of very cold white wine.

White Onion and Corn Chowder

Fry a quarter pound of bacon until crisp; drain off grease. Add half a stick of melted butter and fill the soup pot to a depth of one inch with sliced white onions. Then add two cups of whole corn kernels and about two tablespoons of flour for thickening. Simmer the onions and corn in the butter and flour until they begin to brown, stirring often so the flour doesn't stick to the bottom of the pot. Then pour in a cup of dry white wine and three cups of light cream. Season with sage and salt and white pepper to taste. Cook soup for about forty-five minutes, then run it through the blender for a few seconds on the lowest speed. Sprinkle with chives and serve.

Wine Broth Supreme is a wonderful soup you can make in about fifteen minutes, and for almost any number of people. Just keep adding more ingredients. The amount we will make here will easily serve eight.

Wine Broth Supreme

Cut up into a blender an onion, an apple, a carrot, and a tomato; add a couple of bay leaves, some black pepper, and a couple of tablespoons of moist beef base (or about eight bouillon cubes). Add a couple of cups of chablis (a cheap one will be terrific), grind it all up, and pour it into a soup pot. Add the rest of the fifth of chablis, then add a fifth of cheap red wine (not too dry) and a cup or so of tomato juice (or water, perish the thought); and boil the heck out of it for about fifteen minutes.

Strain it all, pour it back into the pot, bring to a
light boil, and drop in homemade noodles, made as
follows:

Put two eggs into a small bowl and keep stirring in
flour until the mixture is like a very thick syrup.
(The size of your noodles will depend on the thickness of the mixture.) Add a dash of ginger, or marjoram, or whatever you like. Then, with a big
spoon, start stirring your soup in a clockwise direction until you have a whirlpool going on in the soup
pot. Then begin very slowly to dribble in the noodle
mixture. Keep it as close to the side of the pot as you
can—it gives the noodle more room to travel and
cook in the hot broth. If you'd rather have little
dumplings, add about a teaspoonful of baking
powder to the noodle mixture.

**Homemade
Drop Noodles**

   We always serve this soup in a wine glass; but you could put
it in a punch bowl and serve it as a hot punch, or you could chill
it and use it for making the most incredible "bullshot" you've ever
tasted.
   A lot of people have wine glasses sitting around getting dusty
on their shelves because they don't open a bottle of wine every
night. But it's lovely to use wine glasses for juice, sherbet, ice
cream, soup, tea, or just plain ice water. The more comfortable
you feel with nice things, the more nice things will come into your
life.

Appetizers

An appetizer can always be whatever you have the smallest amount of around the kitchen—fish, meat, vegetables, sometimes even flowers. Leftovers make great appetizers; or you can be extravagant and buy something fresh. You can whip up an enormous portion of an appetizer and serve it on crackers or whipped-cream biscuits for a large crowd. Or whatever small amount you might have of anything can be stretched by serving it on toast or biscuits, putting it into a dumpling, or wrapping it up in a piece of cheese—and adding a dab of sour cream or a sauce. (Once you begin to make sauces for your food your life will begin to change. A sauce is simply equal amounts of butter and flour and then whatever you choose to add; you can make it in seconds.)

If you are planning a five-course dinner it's a good thing to have a fish as an appetizer. If you are serving a luncheon, it's wonderful to have a cold vegetable with a hollandaise or cream sauce. There is probably a specific way to make a "true" hollandaise sauce; I have no idea what it is. But the sauce that I call hollandaise is the easiest thing in the world.

Heat about three-quarters of a stick of butter in a saucepan until it's as hot as you can get it before it begins to burn. (If it burns call it a "Burnt Lemon Egg Sauce"—people will be delighted and intimidated.) Then mix in a blender the yolks of four eggs, the juice of one lemon, and a little salt and pepper. While the blender is going slowly pour the hot melted butter into the mixture. (If it curdles add a few drops of white wine or water.) Then pour the smoothed-out egg and butter and lemon back into the saucepan and cook it, stirring the whole time, just until the sides start to become like scrambled eggs. Pour it back into the blender and smooth it out.

Hollandaise Sauce

I never, never fail to get a wonderful, thick, creamy "hollandaise." Once you have the basic sauce down you can begin to feel free to experiment by adding different kinds of herbs and spices. As you simmer the butter, for instance, you can add some sliced shallots, or a clove of garlic, or a leek, an onion, a mushroom, a tomato, some cheese, a hunk of lobster or crabmeat, some watercress...almost anything you happen to have around. Or you could add some heavy cream and a little orange juice concentrate to the blender instead of lemon juice—and absolutely any spice you feel would be appropriate, and maybe a little salt and white pepper.

Somewhere along the way you are bound to hit one of the "classic" sauces by accident; and when someone compliments you on your "perfect Bearnaise," it's really a funny feeling. I once did a dinner where I had made up everything on the menu for the first time. There was a reviewer there that night who came out to the kitchen to talk to me after dinner, and he told me that the only thing he had recognized was the duck. Astonished, I asked him to tell me what he thought was in the duck sauce: giving my imagination free rein, I had mixed figs, oranges, tomatoes, and some Metaxa into a sauce with garlic and butter and a lot of

other things. "Easily," he answered. "It's an old Greek recipe —
tomatoes, oranges, figs, and Metaxa." It just knocked me out.
Well, since there is nothing new under the sun anyway, why
spend a lot of time trying to perfect something you're bound to
hit upon at least once?

Now that you've conquered the hollandaise (or whatever you
want to call it), half your appetizer battle is licked. You can lay
leftover anything on a piece of fresh lettuce and pour a hollandaise over it, and people will talk about it for weeks.

Quail's Eggs in a Green Vodka Sauce

Boil quail's eggs (figure three per person) about
three minutes until hard; a little vinegar in the
water makes the eggs easier to peel. Peel them and
lay them on lettuce leaves. Make a sauce, mixing
one cup of sour cream, a half cup of mayonnaise, a
quarter cup of vodka, one hard-boiled hen's egg, a
handful of chopped chives, and salt and white
pepper to taste. Ladle the sauce over the eggs, top
with a spoonful of caviar, and serve.

Scallops in a Curried Sour Cream and Brandy Sauce

Figure about a handful of scallops per person — if
you're having fifteen people, ask the fish man to
weigh out fifteen handfuls of scallops. (Once you've
done that you'll always know how many pounds will
serve fifteen people. Works the same for everything
else.) Squeeze them in your hands until they are
semi-mashed (make sure you save the juices) and
put them to the side in a mixing bowl. Then slice
about six shallots into a melted stick of butter, "frying" them until they begin to brown. Add a handful
of flour to thicken, stir it well, and add half a glass
of dry white wine, a splash of dry sherry, and a shot
of brandy. Sprinkle in enough mild curry to color
the sauce, some white pepper, a little nutmeg, and
some salt or chicken base. Then add a pint of sour

cream and the juice from the scallops, stir well, and let the sauce simmer for about half an hour. Pour the sauce over the scallops and mix well. Ladle into scallop shells, sprinkle the top with breadcrumbs flavored with lemon juice and butter, and bake at 400° for about twenty minutes. Or you could broil them for about ten minutes.

(Scallops in Curried Sauce)

That's "Scallops in a Curried Sour Cream and Brandy Sauce." It could just as easily be shrimp (slightly boil, clean, and devein your shrimp and then add the sauce), or eel, salmon, swordfish, squid, crabmeat, lobster...whatever. Learn a sauce and then move it around. The sauce will pick up the flavor of whatever you happen to be cooking and taste entirely different from the last time you made it.

The sauce itself can easily change to any number of tastes. Instead of sour cream you can add heavy or light cream; or instead of curry use a little saffron, tarragon, or any spice. You can add lime, lemon, or orange juice, fine-chopped mushrooms, a chopped truffle...the sauce will become a hundred different tastes on a hundred different combinations. Start with the butter and flour and then just keep adding whatever you want. If you prefer a smooth sauce simply blend it for a few seconds.

Lay fillets of salmon on a buttered baking pan and sprinkle with salt, pepper, tarragon, white wine, and lemon juice. Bake at 400° for about twelve minutes, then place in the refrigerator to cool. Into a cup of prepared mayonnaise mix two eggs, a quarter cup of sour cream, a splash of Rose's lime juice, two tablespoons of capers, two sprinkles of tabasco sauce (more depending on how hot you like it), and some white pepper and salt. When the salmon is chilled place each portion on a lettuce leaf, dribble the mayonnaise sauce over it, and

Chilled Salmon in Mayonnaise and Capers Garnished with Quail's Eggs

sprinkle with chopped hard-boiled quail's eggs across the top.

Whipped Cream Shrimp Roll in a Lemon Cheese Sauce

Make a whipped-cream pastry dough (page 134), roll it as thin as you can, and cut it into pieces four inches square. Lay about a third of a cup of cooked shrimp in each one; sprinkle with melted butter, white wine, tarragon, salt, and pepper; and roll them up. Bake at 400° for twelve minutes. Put onto appetizer dishes and cover with a lemon cheese sauce.

Sauce: Mix in a blender one cup of white wine, one cup of grated cheddar cheese, a quarter cup of heavy cream, the juice of one lemon, and salt and white pepper to taste. Blend until smooth, then heat to a light simmer.

Portsmouth Coquille

Mix together in a saucepan twelve ounces of beer, one stick of butter, half a cup of grated Parmesan cheese, six shallots sliced thin, the juice of one lemon, a tablespoon of sweet basil, a teaspoon of oregano, four cloves of garlic sliced thin, a tablespoon each of Worcestershire sauce and A1 sauce, and white pepper to taste. Simmer, stirring often, for at least a half hour while you work with the seafood. Combine in a mixing bowl half a cup of each of the following: fresh peeled and deveined shrimp, king crabmeat, scallops (if large, cut into small pieces), shelled clams, fresh boned salmon, and fresh boned cod. Mix well, then stir the seafood mixture into the sauce. Scoop into baking shells, top with lemon-flavored breadcrumbs, and bake uncovered in a preheated 400° oven for twenty minutes. Serve bubbling.

MUSHROOMS, STUFFED AND OTHERWISE

If you are doing stuffed mushrooms for an appetizer, figure about three mushrooms per person. Wash them, pluck out the stems, lay the mushroom caps on an oiled cookie sheet, and you're ready to stuff them. The basic mushroom stuffing is very simple.

Stuffed Mushrooms

Melt a stick of butter and put it into a mixing bowl; sprinkle generously with garlic powder, pepper, and a dash of olive oil; add a splash of red, white, or rose wine — or dry sherry, or even a little beer. Then mix in enough breadcrumbs to make the mixture like moist sawdust, add a generous pinch of sweet basil and oregano, and stir it very well. Add a couple of handfuls of grated Parmesan cheese (or cheddar or Swiss), mix it together, and taste it. If it seems too dry add a little more melted butter; if it seems too moist simply add more breadcrumbs or cheese. Take a teaspoon and pack stuffing into each mushroom; then bake them at about 400° for twenty minutes to half an hour. When they begin to toast on the top, they are ready.

That's the basic stuffed mushroom. Now you may begin to change it. Stuffed mushrooms can be an incredible fantasy. All you have to do is add a different ingredient to the breadcrumbs. You could chop and fry the mushroom stems, salt and pepper them, and then mix them into the breadcrumbs. Or you could use crabmeat instead of breadcrumbs and just add a handful or so of crumbs to bind it all together. Salmon stuffed mushrooms, crab stuffed, lobster, cheese — it all works on the same principle. Melt the butter and add whatever you like. A couple of spices of your own choosing, the juice of a lemon, a little wine or sherry, some appropriate cheese, and enough breadcrumbs to hold it together. On occasion at Blue Strawbery I use enormous mushrooms, stuff them with chopped lobster tails, pour hollandaise over them, and serve them as an entree. They are fantastic. Stuffed mushrooms are not only an appetizer but can be a canape, a late evening snack, a light luncheon, or a wonderful entree.

Mushrooms and Chestnuts in Chocolate Brandy and Sour Cream

Start with equal amounts of mushrooms and chestnuts. If you can get chestnuts already out of the shell you are in luck. If not, bring about an inch of water to a boil in the bottom of a deep pot, add the chestnuts, and steam them for about fifteen minutes. Drain, then cut them open with a paring knife. Cut the nutmeats in quarters and put them into a mixing bowl. Then slice about three shallots into a frying pan with about three-quarters of a stick of simmering butter, add sliced mushrooms, and fry until they begin to grow limp. Skim the mushrooms into the mixing bowl with the chestnuts, leaving the juices in the frying pan. Then turn the heat up slightly, and add enough flour to the simmering butter to take up half the juices in the pan. Stir well, mixing in by spoonfuls a pint of sour cream—slowly, so that the sauce is smooth and not lumpy. Add salt and white pepper to taste, a couple of sprinkles of tarragon, the rest of the butter—and a good shot of chocolate brandy. Stir well until the sauce bubbles, then mix it with the chestnuts and mushrooms. Pour it into a baking dish or serving-sized souffle dishes and top with grated cheese—Swiss is wonderful, or you can use cheddar or mozzarella. Bake in a 400° oven for twenty minutes to half an hour, and serve bubbling. If you're serving it from a casserole dish, spoon it onto toast or biscuits.

You could probably serve Hamburger and Chestnuts in a Chocolate Brandy Sour Cream Sauce...or rabbit and chestnuts ...or rabbit and almonds...or veal and almonds...or lamb and walnuts...or leave out the nuts and simply mix the sauce with boned pheasant, or chicken breast, or smoked turkey. Or you could change the chocolate brandy to coffee brandy, or experiment with any flavored brandy or liqueur you choose. It's what happens to the mixture of the liqueur and sour cream that matters. It creates a third taste, a new taste that is not at all what you would expect. It's like mixing sour cream and brown sugar — all of a sudden it resembles whipped cream. In this case, with the brandy and sour cream and salt and pepper the taste is not sweet at all, but rich, like a rich gravy. I don't completely understand the chemistry, but I do understand the taste.

Or try baking mushrooms other ways:

Baked Mushrooms in a Wine and Shrimp Sauce

Wash whole mushrooms and place them in a baking dish. Make a sauce of one cup of white wine, half a cup of dry sherry, a tablespoon of chicken base, tarragon, the juice of one lemon, half a stick of melted butter, a little flour for thickening, and salt and white pepper to taste. Simmer the sauce for about half an hour on a low flame, then add a pound of peeled and deveined shrimp. Pour over the mushrooms, cover, and bake in a 400° oven for about twenty minutes. Ladle over toast rounds and serve.

Mushroom Caps Baked in Ricotta and Brandy

Remove the stems from the mushrooms (figure three or four per person) and lay them in a baking dish. Then in a blender mix together half a stick of melted butter, two tablespoons of flour for thickening, one cup of ricotta cheese, a quarter cup of brandy, about half a cup of red wine, and a handful of grated provolone cheese. Season with oregano

(Baked Mushroom Caps) and garlic, blend, and pour over the mushroom caps. Cover and bake at 400° for twenty to thirty minutes. Should make enough to serve six people easily.

ARTICHOKES, AVOCADOS, AND IRISH SALMON

Cold vegetables served as an appetizer are never disappointing. Any green vegetable, simmered until *almost soft* in a little white wine with salt and pepper and a pinch of dill, and served chilled with a dab of hollandaise or sour cream on a lettuce leaf is perfect. But hot or cold, there are so many incredible appetizers you can make with vegetables. On the opening night of Blue Strawbery I made a baked heart of artichoke in a white sauce for an appetizer — inspired by baked hearts of palm in a white sauce I had eaten at the Casa Brasil in New York City. Though I rant about never using canned or frozen or pre-prepared foods, on rare occasions I do buy canned artichoke hearts or hearts of palm. There just are not many palm trees in New Hampshire, and to steam enough artichokes to get to the hearts for eighty people in an evening would drive me crazy. However, almost any supermarket carries canned artichoke hearts, and now and again you can even find a few cans of hearts of palm.

This recipe is named for Dr. and Mrs. Beasley, who always ask if I'm serving the artichokes this way. It's so simple it's almost insulting; and the sauce will work on any hot vegetable you have the courage to try.

Artichokes Beasley Open and drain a can (or two) of artichoke hearts (figure three hearts per person) and lay them on a buttered cookie sheet. Put them into a 400° oven just long enough for them to get hot — about fifteen minutes. Then lay three on each dish, pour the following sauce over, and serve.

Beasley Sauce: Melt a stick of butter in a saucepan, add a handful of flour for thickening, some chicken base, white pepper, a dash of white wine, a few sprinkles of nutmeg, and about a pint of heavy cream. Bring to a boil, smooth it out in a blender, and pour it over the artichokes.

(Artichokes Beasley)

Figuring half an avocado per person, peel, halve, and remove the pits from several ripe avocados. Butter a baking pan and lay salmon fillets on it (probably a quarter pound per avocado half would do it). Sprinkle them with salt, white pepper, lemon juice, white wine, and a little tarragon; and bake them for about twelve minutes. Remove from the oven and cool. Meanwhile with a blender or a spoon mix one cup of mayonnaise, one egg, half a cup of sour cream, a splash or two of Rose's lime juice, the juice of one lemon, a sprinkle each of cayenne pepper, white pepper, salt, and marjoram, a spoon of prepared mustard, and about four shallots slivered. When the salmon has cooled enough, flake it into the mixture, mix well but gently so you don't end with a mush, and fill each one of the avocado halves. Chill before serving.

Avocado Stuffed with Deviled Salmon

There are some flowers that can be dipped in eggs and breadcrumbs and fried in hot butter, then served on toast with a simple butter sauce. Melted butter with the right combinations of ingredients can be a sauce for almost anything. Try melting a stick of butter, slicing in a couple of shallots, adding the juice of a lime, a little salt and pepper, and a pinch of saffron. Then pour that over fried pumpkin blossoms or day lily buds—I guarantee people will begin to talk of your culinary artistry.

Remember that an appetizer should be just that—appetizing. And the more poetic sounding the dish, the more appetizing it will be. Smoked Irish salmon and a frozen papaya custard, to me, is very poetic; and it's not too difficult to make, once you find the imported Irish salmon. (Very expensive, but worth every cent of it. Why can't we make terrific smoked salmon in this country so it wouldn't be so expensive and more people would be able to enjoy it? We have enough smoked pork around to last everyone for the rest of their lives—why aren't people smoking salmon and ducks and goats and rabbit and turtle?)

Smoked Irish Salmon with Frozen Papaya Custard

Slice the Irish salmon and set it aside. (The thinner you slice it, the better it tastes.) Then peel and cut as many papayas as you'll need to fill a blender three-quarters of the way. Add half a small can of frozen orange juice concentrate, the juice of two lemons, a spoon of honey, and enough white wine to cover the whole mixture. Blend until smooth and set aside. Whip a cup of May wine into four egg yolks and two packages of unflavored gelatin and simmer slowly until it begins to form a custard. When the mixture is thick, mix it in the blender with two cups of the papaya, then pour it all back together and stir the egg mixture completely into the rest of the papayas. Set into the freezer for about half an hour. Whip the egg whites until they are almost stiff, take the papaya out of the freezer, put it through the blender one more time, and fold it into the egg whites until the two are perfectly blended. Then cover it and return it to the freezer until it's time to serve. Roll three slices of salmon and stick with a toothpick and a thin wedge of lime. Scoop the papaya custard onto a lettuce leaf or into a champagne glass, and gently lay the impaled Irish salmon across the frozen feast.

It's really the basics of the sherbet that you should concern yourself with. The salmon and papaya could be anything much less expensive and more available. You could do the sherbet with oranges and roll ham across the top; or do the sherbet with plums and use dark chicken meat. Or...you could use mayonnaise instead of a fruit and top it with tuna — boy, if that doesn't sound like something out of a ladies' auxiliary luncheon. Or try making it with mayonnaise and topping it with fresh strawberries, raspberries, or blueberries — a truly lovely dish. Or you could make the custard with cream cheese and serve fresh salmon on it. By and large, the principle of what I call frozen custards is egg yolks cooked with gelatin and wine, mixed with any flavoring and frozen.

FROGS' LEGS

I once saw a cartoon of a small restaurant that advertised frogs' legs: coming out of the back door of the restaurant were several frogs in tiny wheelchairs. But you can't feel guilty about anything you're going to cook and eat; and besides, there is a much easier way to procure frogs' legs — your fish market probably carries them. They are always imported from the Far East, and always frozen. (Once again I have to make allowances for another frozen product.) Frogs' legs, like pajamas, come in three sizes; small and medium are the ones I usually buy, as they cook faster and stay more tender. Large frogs' legs, on the other hand, are sometimes a foot or more in length and begin to resemble cats' legs, or possum legs.

Frogs' Legs in a Tomato and Sherry Sauce

For an appetizer, figure one or two sets of frogs' legs per person (about five sets per person would do for an entree). Thaw them, remove the little cellophane bags and the rubber bands that keep their little legs together, lay them side by side in a baking pan, and pour over the following sauce.

(Frogs' Legs in a Tomato and Sherry Sauce)

Sauce: Melt half a stick of butter, add a little flour for thickening, some garlic, one sliced tomato, a splash of dry sherry, the juice of a lemon, one whole tomato, a little tarragon and basil, some white pepper, and a little chicken base. If you can, mix it in a blender; if not, smash it around as much as possible—the sauce does not have to be smooth. Pour it over the frogs' legs and sprinkle across the top some breadcrumbs mixed with a little melted butter and the juice of a fresh lime. Cover with foil and bake in a 400° oven for about fifteen minutes; uncover and bake another ten. Spoon the frogs' legs onto little dishes, pour a little of the sauce over them, and serve. A wonderful and elegant appetizer.

Instead of a tomato you could put in a spoon of frozen orange juice concentrate; or change the sherry to white wine, or brandy, or cognac, or pernod. The sauce should be not too overwhelming; the frogs' legs are delicate and you really want to taste their flavor. You might also add different spices—saffron, sage, thyme, curry, garlic, anything you might have handy—or you could add tomato juice or cider. Frogs' legs in butter, cider, marjoram, salt, and pepper is outstanding. You can truly add to a butter-and-flour base any combination of ingredients and make a strange and wonderful sauce, using absolutely no recipe.

SWEETBREADS

Whenever I serve sweetbreads at Blue Strawbery there are always a few people who distort their expressions or gag or giggle, or who say, "Uh...no, I'll have the mushrooms." The average diner thinks sweetbreads are the testicles of some animal; not so. Sweetbreads are from the pancreas and the thymus glands along the neck. In every civilized culture they are considered delicacies. They are easy to prepare—but not too easy to procure. If you can buy them fresh you are in luck; if you can get them right off a calf and into a pot, even better.

Sweetbreads are fine for brunch, luncheon, or late night supper—they are even a splendid breakfast, served with champagne and orange juice mixed together. Imagine sitting your out-of-town company down to a breakfast of "Sweetbreads in a Cream Sauce with White Wine and Nutmeg," whipped-cream biscuits with raspberry butter, and an ice-cold pitcher of champagne and orange juice. You could just stay there at the table well along toward lunch time.

Sweetbreads in Cream Sauce with White Wine and Nutmeg

Drop the sweetbreads into boiling water for about ten minutes, then soak them in ice water for at least an hour or two to make it easier for you to remove the membranes and tissues that are attached. This is easy to do—you just pull off the obviously inedible tissue. Then you slice or dice the sweetbread, place it in a casserole, put a sauce over it, and bake. One set of sweetbreads will easily make enough for good portions of an appetizer for six people.

The sauce is simple and wonderful and no trouble at all to fix: Heat up about half a stick of butter, add a spoon of flour for thickening, one small sliced onion, a couple of cubes of beef bouillon, some white pepper, a little summer savory and a dash or two of nutmeg, a splash of dry white wine, and about half a pint to a pint of heavy cream. Pour the sauce over the sweetbreads, sprinkle with some buttered breadcrumbs flavored with a dash of wine or juice, and bake in a 400° oven for twenty to thirty minutes, depending on how large a portion you are making. The breadcrumbs should get a little toasted on top of the sweetbreads; set the dish still bubbling in front of the guests.

Again, the sauce may be anything you choose. It could even be the sauce you just made for the frogs' legs—it tastes entirely different over sweetbreads, or fried chicken livers, or chicken breasts, or baked eel and squid. You will simply be astonished to see how the same sauce reacts to different foods, and how simple it is to be creative in short periods of time investing hardly any energy. Using your imagination is faster, cheaper, and more convenient than convenience foods; you can do anything from scratch in less time than it takes to thaw something out.

SOUFFLES

I didn't eat a souffle until I was twenty-nine years old. It was a chocolate cinnamon souffle that a friend made from a very involved recipe, and it was terrific. I never made one until I was thirty-four years old; but the very first time I made a souffle I made forty at one time, and they all turned out at least three inches over the tops of the dishes. For the first seating at the restaurant I did just the basic cheese souffle. But I was so impressed with their success that by the time the second seating rolled around I was whipping up pumpkin and bacon souffles, and from there on in it just got more and more bizarre.

Souffles are not at all difficult to build. There are a few .things to remember: Be sure your egg whites are not whipped too stiffly, and put a little melted butter into your "sauce"—which is the flavoring and flour and egg yolk that will give the souffle its substance.

Souffle Blue Strawbery

Separate six eggs, putting the whites to one side. Then put one or two of the yolks into a blender with half a stick of melted butter, a splash of dry sherry, a small handful of flour, about a cup of grated cheese, and just enough milk to make the mixture mixable. The choice of seasoning (a little salt and pepper, a spice or an herb, some garlic) and cheese is up to you—almost any combination will work. The mixture should be like a very thick syrup. Whip the egg whites until not quite stiff, but having a loose and creamy texture. Then gently fold the yolk mixture into the egg whites, fill a souffle dish about three-quarters full, and bake at 400° for about thirty minutes. Serves four.

(Souffle)

Souffles are really comparatively easy to make; the basic ingredients are always fluffy egg whites mixed with a thick syrup of one or two egg yolks, flour, and butter. The syrup should be about one-third the amount of egg white; and whatever you choose to mix with the egg yolks and flour and butter will be the thing that decides what the souffle will be. Add a sweet chocolate syrup and a dash of coffee brandy instead of cheese and sherry, and you'll have a Black Mocha Souffle. Or instead of adding a cup of grated cheese, make it half pumpkin, half cheese. Or add a liqueur to the mixture, making apricot or Grand Marnier souffles. . .or collard greens and vodka to make a collard green souffle. Souffles can be made with cooked carrots, broccoli, watercress, pumpkin, squash, squash blossoms, asparagus, or any combination of cooked vegetables. You can also use fruits or combinations of fruits; but they should be cooked a little and drained first, or their juices will make the souffle fall. When the syrup is a little heavier than usual, you can cheat a bit on your souffle and add a teaspoon or so of baking powder—it's not really cheating, it's insurance. And leftover egg yolks can be turned into a sauce, either for the souffle or for some other course.

In the event that your souffle does fall, announce it as a "kouffle"—that's a cross between a souffle and a quiche. A fallen souffle is not really a kouffle, but it comes close enough to be called one. That's why you should never announce your menu before serving each course. If something fails, you can call it another name; people will be most pleased to be eating something "new." But if you have announced you are having a souffle and then it falls, everyone will be most disappointed and you'll be embarrassed to tears.

KOUFFLES

The kouffle, a cross between a souffle and a quiche, is a wonderful appetizer to serve to a lot of people. You bake it in a big pan; if you are serving two dozen people a lasagna-sized pan will do perfectly, or if you are doing it for a few people use a pie tin or any dish that will bake in the oven.

Cheese Kouffle in a Ham Crust

First, you will have to make a "crust." I rarely enjoy making crusts; in this case I grind up about a pound or two of ham and press it with my fingers into the bottom of the pan or dish. Make it as flat and even as possible. Set the crust aside; now for the sauce. Put about two cups of chopped or grated cheese into a saucepan; Swiss cheese is nice, but it could be any kind of cheese, and leftovers work almost better than anything. Add half a cup of white wine, half a cup of light cream, some chives, allspice, garlic, and white pepper; and let it simmer until all the cheese is melted and smooth. Whip up six to eight eggs and slowly blend the cheese mixture into them, making sure it's perfectly blended. Then gently pour it onto the ham base and slip it into a 400° oven for forty-five minutes to an hour. The kouffle is done when a knife inserted into its center comes out clean. Cut it into little squares and serve—hot, warm, room temperature, or even chilled.

The kouffle can become a different dish each time you bake it: vary the spices and cheese you choose, or use brandy or port wine or sherry or anisette instead of white wine. Try not to be afraid to experiment with different and unusual spices and herbs and tastes. We all have a set of taste buds and I think that all of the taste buds should be satisfied. One of the reasons we have such a weight and diet problem in this country is that almost all of the foodstuffs we buy have no tastes. It's as though you haven't eaten anything at all. The more spiced your food, the more satisfying it is to the taste buds — and the more satisfied the taste buds, the less you have to eat and the thinner you remain. Whole, fresh foods rich in taste make an infinitely more healthful diet than some stupid make-believe chocolate or fruit-flavored breakfast drink or lunch square.

CREPES

Someone once told me that the crepe — the thin pancake that can be stuffed with anything edible — was the ultimate fantasy in cooking. I don't know whether I agree, but I do know the crepe to be an instant "solve all" for any serving problem. Not only can the crepe be an appetizer, but also an entire breakfast (imagine strawberry crepes in flaming brandy), a brunch or luncheon (avocado and crabmeat crepes in a sherry cream sauce), or a dinner (lobster stuffed crepes). Often I do an elegant vegetarian crepe — stuffed, for instance, with curried sweet potatoes and leeks in a broccoli and white wine cream sauce.

To make the crepe itself, crack a whole egg into a bowl, then whip in one cup of milk and a half cup of flour, a little melted butter, and a dash of baking powder. Butter the skillet, heated over a moderate flame — I use a large skillet to save time — then pour the extra butter out. Pour about a quarter of a cup of the batter into the center of the frying pan, tilting the pan so that the batter covers the entire bottom

Crepes
Blue Strawbery

(Crepes)   in a thin layer. When the crepe becomes dry on top and golden brown on the bottom, take it off the fire and lay it on a cutting board. Large cool crepes can be cut in quarters to make four separate ones: with the widest part toward you, fill the crepe with about two tablespoons of your stuffing, fold the sides over, then start to roll the crepe, widest part first. Lay the crepes in a baking dish, pour the sauce over them, and bake them at about 450° or 475° for fifteen to twenty minutes and serve.

If you are stuffing your crepes with meat, fish, chicken, or mushrooms, you might add a little salt and spice to the batter. If you are doing sweet crepes add a little sugar or honey to the batter. Crepes stuffed with creamed oysters are always a smash, or you could fill the crepes with any variation on the things we've just made. Try scallops in a curried sour cream and brandy sauce —save a little of the sauce and pour it over the crepes when you are serving them. Or stuff the crepes with stuffed mushrooms— just chop and fry your mushrooms first, mix with the breadcrumb stuffing, fill the crepes and bake; serve with a hollandaise sauce or just plain sour cream. Another good idea is mushrooms and chestnuts in a crepe with a sauce of sour cream and chocolate brandy. Or try artichokes, or sweetbreads inside your crepes. Whatever you might have works fine; you can take chopped chicken, crabmeat, lobster, or just about anything at all, put it in a bowl, add half a stick of melted butter, breadcrumbs, the juice of one lemon, a splash of any liqueur, a little salt, white pepper, and any spice, mix it together, and stuff the crepes. It can't fail. Serve crepes with whatever kind of sauce you want to make. For instance, thicken up some tomato juice with a touch of flour, add a shot of Grand Marnier and a little melted butter, bring to a gentle simmer, and pour over crab stuffed crepes. How could something called "Crepes Stuffed with Crabmeat in a Sauce of Tomato and Grand Marnier" possibly be a disappointment?

BLUE STRAWBERY PARTY CHEESE

There is a very popular French cheese going around these days that truly tastes wonderful. I used it for a while at the restaurant to make sauces but it cost about five dollars a pound and I could easily go through a couple of pounds on a busy night. I knew there had to be a less expensive way to make the sauces than to use that cheese, so I simply made up a cheese of my own using almost the same basic ingredients as the French cheese. I tell you this and will show you how to make that cheese, so that later on in the book (page 94) I can show you how to do salmon in a sauce that I make from that cheese, called Sauce Marguerite. (Marguerite is a lady who's worked for us for the past five years. She is also a vegetarian and claims she doesn't eat anything that has a face—although I did see her licking a clock last week, so think what you will.) Here is how you make Blue Strawbery Party Cheese:

Blue Strawbery Party Cheese

In a saucepan bring to a simmer the following: a quarter cup of chablis, the juice of one lemon, two tablespoons of chives, two teaspoons of white pepper, one tablespoon of garlic powder, one tablespoon of sweet basil, and one teaspoon of marjoram. After you've simmered these ingredients for about ten minutes run them through the blender, then blend them thoroughly into two eight-ounce packages of cream cheese. Set it in the refrigerator to cool.

Use Blue Strawbery Party Cheese on crackers; scoop it onto fresh lettuce and lay a slice of lime and some smoked salmon across the top; fill crepes with the cheese and serve cold. The cheese may vary in many ways. You could use port wine instead of white, chopped onion and caraway and lime juice instead of the other ingredients, and the taste of the cheese will become something else entirely. You can also add the spices to your own taste. Use sherry instead of white wine and cook the yolks of two eggs into the spice mixture, blend it into a smooth custard, mix it into the cream cheese, then into the whipped egg whites, add a cup of heavy cream, and it becomes a topping for cold vegetables or fruits — very wonderful on peaches stuffed with crabmeat or ham. The possibilities are endless. Once again, all you need is a little imagination and some courage to follow it through.

At any rate, those are some basic appetizers that you can turn into whatever you'd like. All are quick and uncomplicated, and require little more than your own imagination. It's a lovely, healthful, and romantic thing to cook something wonderful for people you care about; and the more you cook without recipes the easier it will become. Appetizers are the perfect place to practice.

Salads and Cold Reliefs

The salad is meant to be the "relief" of the dinner. Often it is served after the soup—or second appetizer, if there is one—and very often it is served as the last course of a dinner. Where you serve the salad is up to you, as long as it is crisp, cold, and sports a dressing that gives your taste buds a moment to relax. I must confess I doubt that I've ever made a salad dressing that actually allowed anyone's taste buds to relax, but that's just my style.

A salad can be an entire lunch, dinner, or supper, depending on how much food you put into it. Any large salad for a summer supper is a great idea. There is, of course, the classic Waldorf salad, often seen at the home of the deceased after the funeral: lots of apples and nuts and mayonnaise and whipped cream—always a crowd pleaser at a funeral lunch. There is also the classic chef's salad. This can be an excellent dish; more often, however, it's mundane—slices of julienne ham and cheese and roast beef, an occasional hard-boiled egg, some iceberg lettuce, and a dressing. The dressing is usually French, vinegar and oil, or blue cheese.

I never serve iceberg lettuce at the restaurant, let alone at my own home; it is almost totally water. Romaine is probably the most healthful, hearty lettuce. If you mix it with some chicory, watercress, or endive it can make your salad an event to remember, especially if you're serving only greens and a dressing. Always make sure you've rinsed the lettuce and dried it as much as possible. I am often tempted to buy one of those little plastic machines that spins the water out of lettuce, but it seems like such a luxury that I can't bring myself to part with the ten or fifteen dollars it costs. (Actually, I'm not all that puritanical. If it could do lettuce for forty people at a time I would probably buy one.) Anyway, rinse your lettuce under very cold water and shake it dry, or pat it gently with a tea towel or, God forbid, paper towels. (I never buy paper towels anymore.)

Everything that goes into the salad should be ice-cold—the greens, the dressing, cold vegetables, cold meats, fish, or fruit. Whatever goes in, the crowning glory of every salad is the dressing. All dressings begin with vinegar and oil; then you add whatever you have a taste for. If you make too much dressing just bottle it and keep it in the refrigerator.

Following is a list of salad dressings and how to make them according to your own taste. I use a blender for almost all the dressings. If you don't have a blender, put the ingredients into a jar and shake it well. I could give you the precise measurements for the dressings but it would all be to my taste. Besides, if you follow precise measurements you'll never experiment, and if you don't experiment you'll never learn to rely on your own taste.

It's always nice to make a lot of salad dressing; the amounts in the following descriptions will yield enough to serve six people easily with plenty left over for yourself the next day.

Sour Cream and Roquefort Dressing

The longer this dressing sits, the funkier it becomes. It's wonderful on all salads, but especially on tomatoes by themselves, or cucumbers. To three-fourths cup vinegar add one and a half cups oil, one pint of sour cream, a handful of chopped chives, some white pepper, two cloves of garlic, dashes of sweet basil and marjoram, the juice of one lemon, and eight ounces of Roquefort cheese. Blend lightly just until all the ingredients are mixed. If it's a little lumpy from the cheese that's fine. Blue cheese might be used, or Gorgonzola, or you could change the properties of the dressing altogether by adding cheddar or Swiss or any other cheese you might want to try.

(Sour Cream and Roquefort Dressing)

Three-fourths cup vinegar to one and a half cups oil. Then add a small can of tomato puree, the juice of one lemon, a handful of grated Parmesan cheese, some celery seed, a little dill, black pepper, and a nice spoon of honey. (You could use brown sugar, and the Parmesan could be any cheese you like or happen to have around.) If the dressing seems too tart you might add a little more tomato or sugar or oil — that will dilute it. If you want more tartness add more lemon juice, lime juice, or vinegar.

French Dressing Blue Strawbery

Mix in a blender one cup of cooked peas, half a cup of white vinegar, one cup of oil, a spoonful of prepared mustard, dill, white pepper, and about a tablespoon of grated Parmesan cheese.

Pea Vinaigrette

Three-fourths cup vinegar, one and a half cups oil, one whole egg, a large handful of fresh cranberries, the juice of two limes, a couple of squirts of catsup, a little celery seed, salt and pepper, and enough honey or sweetening to bring it just over the point of being tart.

Cranberry Lime Dressing

Blue Cheese Egg Lime Dressing

Three-fourths cup vinegar, one and a half cups oil, black pepper to taste, the juice of two limes, one egg, and a six-ounce package of blue cheese.

Egg White and Herb Dressing

Four egg whites, three-fourths cup vinegar, one and a half cups oil, some summer savory, a little dill, basil, chives, salt and pepper to taste. Blend until creamy.

Orange and Yogurt Dressing

Three-fourths cup vinegar, one and a half cups oil, half an orange with peelings, half a pound of yogurt, salt, pepper, celery seed, and a good glob of honey. Puree until the orange is smoothed into the yogurt.

Orange and Blue Cheese Dressing

Three-fourths cup tarragon vinegar, one and a half cups oil, a small package of blue cheese, half an orange with peelings, celery seed, white pepper and salt. Blend until smooth.

Mango Dressing

Mix in the blender half a cup of vinegar, one and a half cups oil, a quarter cup of Rose's lime juice, two peeled mangoes, salt and pepper, garlic, and a dash of sage.

Tomato Lime Dressing

Three-fourths cup vinegar, one and a half cups oil, half a lime with peelings, one small can of tomato paste, some salt, white pepper, dill, and basil, and about three ice cubes. Whip it quickly in a blender until frothy. Try it on chilled artichoke hearts, hearts of palm, or Boston Bibb lettuce. Or fill the center of a cantaloupe with sliced chicken breast and pour this dressing over it.

Mix the usual three-fourths cup vinegar (cider vinegar is nice in this dressing) and one and a half cups oil (soy oil mixes well), a good handful of brown sugar, a small onion, some garlic, and a little salt and pepper. Jiggle this dressing around; taste it often. It should never taste sweet; though it is a sweet and sour dressing, I prefer it more sour than sweet. The brown sugar should only hang in the background—like a nuance, a memory.

Sweet and Sour Brown Sugar Dressing

Instead of three-fourths cup vinegar, use half vinegar and the other half an equal combination of lemon juice and Rose's lime juice. Add three-fourths cup oil, a good handful of grated Parmesan cheese, a handful of chives, some white pepper, a little salt, and a cup of yogurt. It's best on chilled, sliced cucumbers.

Lime and Yogurt Parmesan Cream

In a blender mix for a few seconds at low speed three-fourths cup vinegar (an imported French tarragon vinegar would be nice), three-fourths cup pure olive oil, three-fourths cup soy oil, a good spoonful of Dijon mustard, some white pepper, the juice of one lemon, two crushed garlic cloves, one egg that has sat in boiling water for one minute, and a dash of Escoffier Diable sauce. In the classic Caesar you would here add a small can of anchovy fillets, and then the sauce would be done. I omit the anchovies, however, blend the dressing, pour it into a bowl, and then slowly stir in three to four ounces of caviar.

Caviar Caesar

COLD RELIEFS

You would be amazed at how few people think of serving something other than greens for a salad when there are so many wondrous reliefs to delight the palate. Fresh fruits or vegetables in a simple and imaginative sauce, or homemade sherbets flavored with wine or liqueur provide a refreshing pause in an elegant dinner.

Cranberry Orange Wine Sherbet

In a blender mix up two cups of whole cranberry sauce with one small can of frozen orange juice concentrate, one whole orange with half the peelings, two cups of chablis, a shake of cardamom, and just enough milk to lighten it a shade. Pour it into a baking pan and set it in the freezer for about an hour, take it out and whip it with an electric beater, right in the pan, then return it to the freezer and let it stay until it sets. Cover it with tin foil or something to keep the top from crystallizing.

Cranberry Orange Wine Sherbet is very lovely served as a relief between a collard green quiche and a chicken breast stuffed with smoked salmon in an asparagus and white wine cream sauce. (If you wanted to build the entire dinner around the sherbet you would start with Wine Broth Supreme, then the collard green quiche, the sherbet, the stuffed chicken breast, and parsnips flambee in oranges and curry and apricot brandy. And for dessert, serve fresh strawberries for dipping in sour cream and brown sugar. To make that menu for some ordinary Tuesday evening would make the event unforgettable.) Or serve the sherbet as a punch with a lot of champagne poured over it; or for breakfast in a scooped-out melon; or as a dessert in a wine glass with a liqueur poured over it.

Mix in a blender four each of peeled oranges, lemons, and limes, two large cans of frozen orange juice concentrate, one small bottle of Rose's lime juice, four small cans of frozen cranberry juice concentrate, a fifth of burgundy, and half a quart of black cherry soda. Whip it all together, let it freeze, whip it again, and place it back in the freezer for another hour or two until it freezes up. Serve in burgundy glasses.

Burgundy Punch Sherbet

Mix in a blender the meat from one melon (cantaloupe, honeydew, or Cranshaw), one cup of cran-apricot juice, half a cup of Rose's lime juice, the juice of two lemons, and about a cup of honey. It should not be too sweet, but on the tart side. Blend until smooth, pour into trays, and freeze. Serve scooped into champagne or burgundy glasses. Serves six.

Summer Snow

Put into a blender one whole lime, one small container of frozen orange juice concentrate, two small containers of frozen limeade concentrate, a pinch of sweet basil, about half a cup of honey, one cup of milk, a small bottle of Rose's lime juice, and the juice of two lemons. Puree until smooth, blend it into eight cups of applesauce, and freeze it for about two hours. Take it out, whip it again, and refreeze until it's time to serve. The amounts given will make enough sherbet to serve at least eight people. It should be very tart—this sherbet is wonderful with cold pork or cold smoked fish, or as a relief to any dinner, or by itself.

Lime Applesauce Sherbet

**Melon
Sherbet**

Scoop the meat from four ripe melons—Cranshaw, Peruvian, honeydew, cantaloupe, or whatever melon you happen to have handy. Put it in a blender with the juice of two limes and four lemons, a couple of cups of apple juice, and half a cup of honey. Blend until smooth, put it into the freezer for an hour or so, blend again, and return it to the freezer until time to serve.

**Asparagus
Meringue**

Mix one cup of chopped cooked drained asparagus, three-fourths cup vinegar and three-fourths cup oil, the juice of one lime, some salt, and white pepper. Blend until smooth and gently fold it into seven egg whites that have been beaten until stiff. Heap it on fresh raw spinach that has been washed and trimmed. Serves six.

**Orange Slices
in Chocolate Brandy**

Separate enough orange slices to feed six people and place them in a large bowl. In a blender mix half a cup of hot melted butter, two cinnamon sticks, a cup of chocolate brandy, and a small can of frozen orange juice concentrate. Whip well, stir over the oranges, and let sit overnight, covered, in the refrigerator. Serve in champagne glasses. Excellent with smoked breast of turkey.

**Grapefruit Slices
in Brandy
and Honey**

Slice as much grapefruit as you'll need into a bowl and cover with equal amounts of honey and brandy that have been blended with two cinnamon sticks and a dash of cardamom. Let sit until well chilled and serve on a lettuce leaf, in a champagne glass, or over chocolate ice cream for dessert.

**Cucumbers
in Bacon Chive
Sour Cream**

Score the cucumbers and slice them as thin as you possibly can into a mixing bowl. Slowly blend in a pint of sour cream. (If you use six cucumbers you will have enough to serve ten people easily.) Then mix in half a pound of crisp crumbled bacon spiced with salt, pepper, and garlic, and splashed with apricot brandy. Sprinkle in a good handful of chopped chives, a little salt, and white pepper. This dish should not be made up too long in advance as the cucumbers will eventually leak into the sour cream and make the sauce runny.

(Cucumbers in Bacon Chive Sour Cream)

Score several cucumbers (figure one for every two people) and cut into thin slices. Then mix half a cup of vinegar, half a small can of frozen orange juice concentrate, one cup of oil, and the juice of one lemon. Season this sauce with salt, pepper, and dill; and pour over the cucumbers. Chill and serve.

Cucumbers in an Orange Vinaigrette

Cut a large Cranshaw melon into eight pieces, then spoon the iced sauce over it and serve.

Sauce: In a blender mix a dozen pitted nectarines and a shot each of apricot brandy, red Dubonnet, Grand Marnier, chartreuse, anisette, creme de menth, and chocolate brandy, half a cup of sweet vermouth, one whole lemon with peelings, and a dash of cardamom. Whip until smooth and place in ice trays to freeze. When it has frozen around the edges whip it again and set it back to freeze. Let it sit for about two hours in the freezer, blend it again, and pour over the melon. It should be like a frozen sauce.

Cranshaw Melon with a Nectarine Liqueur Sauce

Peel and slice equal amounts of as many mangoes and nectarines as you'll need into a mixing bowl. Then, in a blender, mix together one whole orange with peelings, half a lime with peelings, a dash or two of cardamom, one pound of natural yogurt, a

Mangoes and Nectarines in a Liqueur and Yogurt Sauce

cup of any liqueur you have handy, and a couple of spoonfuls of honey.

Midsummer Fruit

Cut into bite-sized pieces as many kinds of fresh fruit as you can find. Then, in a blender, mix a cup of brandy, two cups of whole cranberry sauce, a cup of red wine, a small can of frozen orange juice concentrate, one whole lemon, and a little cardamom. Blend until smooth, pour over the fruit, and chill for a couple of hours. Ladle into champagne or wine glasses and serve.

Mixed Fruit in a Roquefort Meringue

Cut enough plums, mangoes, and green tomatoes into bite-sized pieces and set aside. Then whip into stiff peaks the whites of eight eggs and slowly fold into them the following sauce: one four-ounce package of Roquefort cheese, some dill, a little white pepper, and about a cup of sour cream. Fold the fruit into the seasoned meringue and serve in champagne glasses or little glass bowls, or on a lettuce leaf.

Watermelon in Orange Juice and Beer

Remove all the seeds from as much watermelon as you need to serve, cut it into bite-sized pieces, place it in a bowl, and pour over it a large can of frozen orange juice concentrate and enough beer to cover the melon. Let sit until well chilled and serve. It will be a great surprise.

Belgian Endive in a Chive Whipped Cream

In the blender mix one eight-ounce package of cream cheese with a splash of vinegar, a handful of chives, the juice of two lemons and one lime, a splash of dry white wine, one garlic clove, one very small onion, and a good handful of grated Parmesan cheese. Blend until perfectly smooth. Heat up a quarter cup of white wine and melt two envelopes of unflavored gelatin in it, then add it to the above mixture. Whip up two pints of whipping cream, and blend in the cheese and chive mixture. Put a couple of tablespoons of the chive whipped cream into the bottom of a champagne glass and arrange five leaves of the Belgian endive in the center like a lotus leaf. Set in the refrigerator to chill for an hour or so before serving. It should, of course, be eaten with the fingers, each leaf dipped into the cream. If you like, use pimientos instead of or in addition to the chives.

(Belgian Endive)

Chop equal amounts of apples and cucumbers, leaving the peelings on, put them into a bowl, and set aside to chill. In a blender mix the following: three-fourths cup vinegar, one and a half cups oil, a small bottle of Rose's lime juice, salt and white pepper, sweet basil, the juice of a lemon, and a dash of sugar. Blend until smooth, then freeze. When the mixture is well frozen crush it into the apples and cukes and serve immediately.

**Apples
and Cucumbers
in a Frozen Dressing**

There is probably no combination of fruits, vegetables, lettuce, and dressings that will not work as a relief to the rest of the meal. All of the above ideas can be easily changed into whatever is the most convenient for you to make. All you really need is an adventuresome appetite and a little courage.

Meat

There are four choices for any entree: meat, fowl, fish, or vegetable. Although it's advisable—from the standpoint of economy as well as health—to steer clear of too much beef, it will probably continue to be part of the American way of life. Since it is also a delicious meat I feel it only fair to pass along to you a few of the tricks that keep me from making failures from expensive cuts of beef.

Tenderloin of Beef is often referred to as Chateaubriand. It's expensive, and should be cooked quickly in a hot oven.

Tenderloin of Beef   Figure about a third of a pound of meat per person. Peel the fat off the top, and cut off the tail. (You can grind the tail into very elegant hamburger, or slice it thin and make a stroganoff with it.) Never salt beef before you cook it: it's the surest way to make it tough; but before you place the tenderloin in the oven it's nice to pepper it and spice it—with some garlic, or lemon juice, or a bay leaf or two.

Preheat the oven to 500°; put the tenderloin into a baking pan (just lightly greased if you feel you must: I never grease a pan when I'm cooking meat, except with bacon to keep it from shrinking too much), and place it in the oven to bake. I allow about ten minutes to the pound, or even less, until the meat is a deep rare pink; all meat and ovens are different, and you'll have to learn to judge when it's ready by the smell and the feel of the meat. (It's no feat of magic; cook one and you'll immediately get the idea.) When it's done, let it sit for about five minutes before you cut and serve it. That lets the juices settle down inside the meat, making it even more tender and flavorful. Slice the meat on an angle (it creates the illusion of a larger piece), lay it on a serving platter, and pour a simple sauce over the top.

(Tenderloin of Beef)

The most simple sauce is made by simmering some mushrooms in red wine, and adding a little beef base, a bay leaf or two, one tomato cut up, a little savory, marjoram, basil, and garlic, an onion chopped fine, a little flour for thickening, a couple of sliced shallots, and some black pepper. I would mix everything but the mushrooms in a blender until smooth, pour it into a saucepan, add the mushrooms, and let it sit and simmer for an hour or so.

Prime rib should be cooked with a layer of fat on the top, the bones on the bottom. The fat on top will make it more tender and flavorful; especially if you reach under the layer of fat and put in a couple of bay leaves and a little garlic before putting the prime ribs into the oven. The oven should be very hot: preheat it to 500° or 525°. Cook the roast in a good-sized baking pan; a ten-pound rib roast takes

Prime Rib of Beef

(Prime Rib of Beef)

about two hours and fifteen to twenty minutes. If it begins to smoke a lot, just drain off the grease and return it to the oven.

When the prime rib roast is done you can stand it on its side and slice off a piece at a time. But I always remove the fatty top of the ribs; then with a sharp knife I cut along the back of the bone underneath the meat and remove the bone. (This makes it much easier to carve, and I think the meat tends to go a little further. All you're really doing is trimming the meat so your guests won't have to.) What you have left is the "eye" of the beef. Slice this at any thickness you choose, lay it on a platter, and pour an appropriate sauce over the meat. A wonderful sauce for prime rib of beef is Sparkling Burgundy and Artichoke Sauce, from page 99.

The less expensive cuts of beef for roasting—known as chuck roasts, rolled roasts, and any number of other names—must be cooked longer; they can be very tough if served rare. I think the most memorable roast—and a very American dish—is a baked pot roast. Easy to prepare:

Baked Pot Roast Blue Strawbery

Put a little grease (oil, lard, or bacon grease) in the bottom of a roasting pan, and heat it almost until it begins to smoke. Put the roast into a paper bag with about a cup of flour and shake it well to completely coat it with flour; this makes the gravy easier to prepare. Then brown the roast on all sides in the hot grease on top of the stove; watch the heat so the flour doesn't burn. Pepper the meat and lay a couple of bay leaves, some marjoram, and a sliced onion across its top; then cover it and put it in the oven at 500°. After fifteen minutes, turn the oven down to about 400°; and while the roast is cooking

peel some carrots, wash some potatoes, and wash
and snap some fresh green beans. When the meat
has cooked for an hour, turn it over, spice the other
side as you did the first, then lay the carrots,
potatoes, and beans separately in the roasting pot.
On the carrots it's nice to sprinkle a little sugar, salt,
and pepper; on the potatoes and beans some salt,
pepper, and a little sweet basil. Add a couple of
cups of wine or beer, and let it bake for another
hour. For the last fifteen minutes of that hour you
should take the cover off the roasting pan; stir the
juices around, make sure nothing is sticking to the
bottom of the pot, and baste all the vegetables. It's
nice if the vegetables begin to brown on the top a
little. When the roast is done, put it on the table
and serve; the gravy is already there.

**(Baked
Pot Roast)**

If you feel there is too much grease in the gravy, or if you'd
like the gravy to be thicker, just remove the meat and vegetables
from the juice and let it sit for a few moments. The grease will
rise to the top and you can just skim it off. If you want to stretch
the gravy, beat in a little moist beef base and flour and add a
little more wine, or water, or even light cream to the juices.
There should be enough gravy from a six-pound roast easily to
soak all the potatoes.

VEAL

Veal is the meat from the young steer or calf. It should always be
cooked until well done; it is much too tough when rare. Veal is
elegant; no other word can describe it. It can be fixed many
wonderful ways (it comes in various forms—legs, shoulders,
cutlets, chops, loin) and it's such a delicate meat that it easily
takes herbs and spices, or cream and wine sauces. Even vegetables
made into cream sauces work best on veal.

Veal is usually very expensive; though occasionally you can get veal legs on sale for relatively little. There is little fat on a leg of veal; if you want more grease you can lay a few strips of bacon over the meat before you cook it. The way I'm going to tell you to do a leg of veal, though, gives you the juiciest possible meat.

Leg of Veal in a White Wine and Allspice Cream Sauce

Preheat the oven to 450°. Rub the veal down with salt, pepper, garlic, lemon juice, and butter; lay it in a baking pan, uncovered, and let it cook for half an hour. Then cover it and let it cook forty-five minutes; uncover it, pour your sauce over the roast, cover it again and cook another half hour; uncover and let it cook another fifteen minutes. Altogether, it will have cooked for two hours. Don't worry about exactly when you do the different steps; if you just do it when you remember, it'll still work out.

While the veal is roasting, you should be putting the sauce together. Saute shallots in butter and thicken with flour. Then add about a cup of dry white wine, a pint of heavy cream, some salt and white pepper, and a little allspice. Simmer about twenty minutes, until it begins to get thick — add a little flour if it's not thick enough, and run it through the blender if it needs smoothing out. Then slice the veal onto a platter and pour the sauce over. The combination of veal and wine and cream and allspice will present you with one of the most simple and different tastes you've ever experienced.

This particular sauce can be the basis for many other sauces merely by adding to the existing ingredients a couple of cups of any of the following: chopped broccoli, chopped watercress, chopped pumpkin, tomatoes, crabmeat, mushrooms, carrots, artichoke hearts, cheese, langostinos, or lobster meat.

That is the basic way to prepare a leg of veal: two hours in the oven at 450°, covered and uncovered, and pour a sauce over it. Veal cutlets are equally simple, but they are done very differently and don't take nearly as much time. Cutlets are a more expensive cut of meat, but don't let that frighten you away—in a pound you might get four to six nice cutlets.

The most simple way of preparing veal cutlets is this: Heat equal amounts of butter and oil to cover the bottom of a frying pan. Dip the veal cutlets in flour and lay them in the hot grease. Salt and pepper and spice them, and let them cook about five minutes until they brown. Then turn them, salt and pepper them again, sprinkle the juice of one lemon over them, and let cook until they brown on that side—then serve. That's the basic method; you might splash a little white wine on them along with the lemon juice, or sprinkle them with almonds or Parmesan cheese.

**Veal
Cutlet**

I call the next dish "Veal Willhauk" after George and Mary Willhauk who eat at Blue Strawbery almost as much as I do. It is cutlet of veal in a pumpkin sauce under a cheese and pumpkin souffle—true American cuisine, as the pumpkin is indigenous to North America.

Start with as many veal cutlets as you'll need to serve —two apiece if they are really small, one good-sized one otherwise. Bread them in eggs and cracker or bread crumbs with a little Parmesan cheese added to the crumbs. Fry them very quickly, just until they brown on the outside, then lay them in a baking dish. Lay slices of Swiss cheese (or any cheese you have handy) across the cutlets, pour the pumpkin sauce over the cheese, and then gently lay the pumpkin meringue over the sauce. Bake in a 400°

**Veal Cutlet
in a Pumpkin Sauce
under a Cheese
and Pumpkin
Souffle**

(Veal in Pumpkin under Souffle)

oven for about thirty minutes, and serve right from the baking dish at the table.

Pumpkin Sauce: In a saucepan brown a handful of sliced shallots in a stick of butter, watching so that it doesn't burn. Thicken with half a cup of flour, and add some white pepper, a good tablespoon of moist chicken base, some tarragon, a little soy sauce, about two cups of white wine, and two cups of cooked pumpkin. (If you are cooking the pumpkin from scratch, split the pumpkin in half, clean out the seeds, and bake at 400° for almost an hour, depending on the size of the pumpkin. Poke it around now and then; you'll soon discover when it's done.) Simmer the pumpkin mixture for almost an hour on a very low flame, stirring often. When you're ready to put the veal into the oven, blend up a cup of heavy cream with four egg yolks, fold this mixture smoothly into the pumpkin sauce, and pour three-quarters of the sauce over the cheese and veal. Into the quarter that's left, mix one cup of grated sharp cheddar (or any other good sharp cheese). Then, gently and gradually, fold the pumpkin-cheese mixture into eight egg whites that have been whipped just until soft peaks begin to form. (If you whip the whites until stiff they will be unable to expand further. They need to be able to expand with the aid of the oven's heat.) Lay this mixture gently across the top of the veal, cheese, and sauce, place it in a 400° oven, and bake it for about forty minutes. I guarantee you will be astonished.

Of course, the sauce for the veal cutlets could be made several different ways. Instead of pumpkin, you could use apple slices, substituting sour cream for the heavy cream. Or instead of pumpkin you could use chunks of crabmeat in the sauce, changing the white wine to a very dry, light sherry. Substitute any new ingredient for the pumpkin and you've got a totally different dish. I'm still trying to apply that to other areas of my life — it sounds so logical and kind of esoteric — but so far it only works in the kitchen. Maybe I'm not sure what the main ingredient is.

LAMB

Like veal, lamb all comes in just about the same size. This is because if it gets bigger than a certain size it is called mutton, and if it is smaller, it simply is not profitable to sell. It's safe to say, therefore, that you cook a leg of lamb for almost two hours, give or take fifteen minutes.

In Spain, I have heard, they put a lot of olive oil and garlic and pepper and bay leaves on a leg of a fresh-killed lamb and throw it into a red-hot brick oven, searing the meat to save all the juices. It sounds like a terrific way to cook a leg of lamb, but a little difficult in homes without red-hot brick ovens. Try to come as close as possible by this method:

Roast Leg of Lamb in an Orange, Tomato, Red Wine, and Pepper Sauce

Turn the oven to its highest point and give it a good twenty minutes, without opening the door, to preheat. Rub the lamb down with a mixture of a half cup each of melted butter and pure olive oil, spiced with lemon juice, mustard, garlic, pepper, sage, and salt. Lay the meat in a baking pan and quickly thrust it into the quivering white oven, trying to lose as little heat as possible. It will probably smoke a lot; you can try to alleviate this by draining off the excess grease, or you can just live through it. After about forty-five minutes pour a bottle of white wine over the leg of lamb and cover. Return it to the oven, turn the heat down to 400°, and bake another forty-five minutes, meanwhile starting to prepare

(Lamb in Orange, Tomato, Red Wine, and Pepper)

the sauce. Then take the lamb out of the oven and drain the juices into the sauce you are preparing. Pour the sauce over the lamb and return it to the oven, uncovered, for about twenty or thirty minutes, depending on size and degree of doneness. Meat from a young fresh lamb should be a little on the rare side. When the lamb is done remove it from the pan and slice it into servings, lay them on a platter, pour the sauce over, and serve. If the sauce appears to have too much butter in it, put it through a blender; adding a dash of flour or the yolk of an egg will bind it a little more.

Orange, Tomato, Red Wine, and Pepper Sauce: Melt half a stick of butter in a saucepan, and add about six sliced shallots, two leeks, one small onion, one sliced orange with peel, two cups of stewed plum tomatoes (with their juice), whatever you think is a lot of garlic, the juice from one lemon, and a few hot peppers cut into long strips. Add four cups of very dry red wine, salt to taste, and simmer for half an hour. Mix in the juices from the roasting meat, and pour over the lamb.

We rarely ate lamb when I was growing up in the Midwest; but the more often I serve leg of lamb the more I appreciate its taste. One way I've done this is to think of as many things as I can that sound exotic with lamb. You could make the above sauce using all apricots, three cups of orange juice, a cup of brandy, and perhaps a little saffron. Could you possibly resist "Leg of Lamb Roasted in a Sauce of Apricots and Metaxa," served after an appetizer of collard greens stuffed with rice and chicken livers, sauteed in white wine?

Cream sauces also work beautifully on lamb dishes. Instead of oranges and tomatoes you could add a cup of cream and a cup of pimientos, and blend it until it becomes creamy. Then pour it over the lamb and bake.

Sometimes it's easier to slice the cooked lamb and place it in a baking and serving dish before pouring the sauce over it. The effect is just as nice, and you don't have to stand around slicing in front of everyone when it's time to sit down and eat.

Bake the lamb as suggested above, meantime preparing a sauce as follows. Melt a stick of butter in the bottom of a saucepan with two tablespoons of flour for thickening. Slice in about four shallots and two leeks, and add some sage, black pepper, thyme, a quarter cup of soy sauce, a quarter cup of honey, two tablespoons of catsup, two tablespoons of moist beef base, and a teaspoon each of nutmeg and dry mustard. Then blend one cup of uncooked pumpkin meat with one cup of red wine and half a cup of cognac. Pour into the leek sauce and let simmer slowly for half an hour.

When it's time to drain the grease from the baking lamb, pour the sauce over the meat and bake covered for another half hour. Then uncover and bake fifteen more minutes. Serve.

Roast Leg of Lamb in a Pumpkin, Honey, and Soy Sauce

PORK

Pork in any form should be cooked until well done — it should almost be overdone. If it's pink put it back in the pan. Pork may be baked, fried, stuffed, sauteed, or roasted. Served cold it's a triumph; and the meat works equally well with fruit and with vegetables.

My favorite cut is probably roast loin of pork; it is a good meat for the money. One of my most vivid childhood memories is of my grandmother cooking a pork roast with a dark, rich, wonderful brown gravy with onions, and with plenty of mashed potatoes on the side to pour the gravy on. I usually cook a large pork roast for about three hours, until it's almost falling apart.

Probably the most popular pork dish I make is Roast Loin of Pork in White Wine, Mushrooms, Sour Cream, and Sauerkraut; it really is a knockout.

Roast Loin of Pork in White Wine, Mushrooms, Sour Cream, and Sauerkraut

Preheat the oven to 500° for at least fifteen minutes. Season the roast generously with salt, black pepper, bay leaves, marjoram, and garlic; also slice an onion and lay it across the fatty top of the roast. The bones should be on the bottom. Bake the roast uncovered for about forty-five minutes, draining off some of the grease if it smokes too much. At the end of this period, drain all the grease off and pour half a fifth of chablis over the top of the roast. Then cover it and return it to the oven, which you should turn down to 400°. After another forty-five minutes or so, drain off the juices and skim the grease off, leaving just the rich, winey, brown pork gravy. Mix this juice into the sauce, pour it all over the pork, cover again, and return it all to the oven for another forty-five minutes. Then uncover and let 'bake another fifteen minutes. Slice onto a platter, pour the sauce over, and serve.

Sauce: Melt half a stick of butter and add about half a cup of flour for thickening. Then add a handful of sliced shallots, the other half of the fifth of chablis, a handful of drained sauerkraut, two pints of sour cream, and fresh mushrooms (sliced, crumbled, or whole). Spice to taste with salt, white pepper, garlic, marjoram, basil, a couple of bay leaves, and a dash of Parmesan cheese. Stir well and let simmer for forty-five minutes to an hour. Add the skimmed pork gravy, stir well, pour over the roast, and bake as above.

When it comes time to serve the roast, if the sour cream sauce seems to have too much pork grease in it just skim it off as best you can. If the sauce seems to have separated, you can strain out the mushrooms and smooth the sauce in the blender, adding a little flour if it is too thin. Or you might simply stir the sauce quickly with a fork or whisk.

(Roast Pork)

Again, it's the way the roast is cooked that should be remembered; the sauce can be altered in whatever way you wish. You could leave the sour cream out of the sauce altogether, and use red wine and onions and mushrooms and sauerkraut; or you could leave the sauerkraut out. Or leave out the sauerkraut and make the sauce with sour cream and apricots and white wine. All fruit goes well with pork.

Trim the fat off two inch-thick pork chops for each person you plan to serve, lay them in a baking dish, season them with salt and pepper, and bake them uncovered at about 475° for fifteen minutes. Cover them and bake another twenty minutes. Take them out of the oven, drain off the grease, and then spread over the chops five cored and sliced apples, half a cup of honey, and two cups of a dry white wine; sprinkle the chops generously with allspice. This is a lovely and easy dish to prepare.

Baked Pork Chops with Apples, White Wine, and Honey

Place the chops in a baking pan and season with salt, pepper, and ginger. Bake them uncovered in a 475° oven for about twenty minutes, and then drain off the grease. Slice enough apples across the chops to cover them, then cover them again with grated cheddar cheese and one good cup of cream sherry. Sprinkle lightly with allspice, cover, and return to the oven. Turn the heat down to 400° and bake about half an hour.

Baked Pork Chops in Apples, Sherry, and Cheddar Cheese

In order to make the best stuffed pork chops get them cut thick enough so that there are two bones on each chop. You make the cut in the back of the chop, between the two bones (your butcher can do this for you), and fill the little pocket. Bake them with the bones up in the pan so the stuffing doesn't fall out or become soaked in pork grease.

Baked Pork Chops Stuffed with Brandied Apricots in a Sour Cream Sauce

Cut thick pork chops in the back, between the two bones, to make a pocket. Soak a cup of dried apricots, or about eight fresh ones, in apricot brandy for at least a couple of hours; the brandy should cover the fruit. If you have fresh apricots, pit them but don't peel them — the peel adds a terrific flavor of its own. Then drain off the brandy and set it aside. Place the apricots in a bowl, add half a stick of melted butter, one egg, some salt and white pepper, and just enough breadcrumbs to hold it all together. Pack the stuffing into the chops, and lay them in a baking pan with the bones and stuffing up. Season the meat with salt, pepper, and sweet basil, and bake, uncovered, in a preheated 450° oven for about half an hour. Then drain off the grease, pour the sauce over, and bake covered at 400° for another half hour. Take the cover off, baste with the sauce, and bake for another fifteen to twenty minutes. Serve.

Sauce: Mix about half a stick of melted butter with a couple of sliced shallots and about half a cup of flour for thickening. Add a pint of sour cream and the juice from the apricot brandy marinade. Season with white pepper and thyme.

Baked pork chops can be stuffed with anything you'd like — brandied apples, grapefruit, oranges, plums, or peaches are all wonderful; or make a vegetable or bread stuffing instead of fruit.

You could make a stuffing with zucchini and celery soaked in white wine; or a stuffing of chopped celery, breadcrumbs, and a little pork sausage; or mix apples with pork sausage. It's endless and easy. All you have to do is omit the thing you don't want, and replace it with whatever you do want—it's incredible how it happens to work out. That's why I always say that you should feel as loose as possible about whatever you're cooking. Make as many logical changes as you feel you want: you're creating, not doing a classical recipe.

Pork Cutlets are made from the tenderloin of pork, which is probably my favorite bit of meat. The way I like them best of all is dipped in eggs and breadcrumbs and fried slowly in a half-and-half mixture of oil and butter, and topped with a lemon-egg sauce, cheese sauce, cream sauce, or wine sauce. Pork is a rich meat; the rest of the dinner should be a little on the light side. You might serve baked apples in cranberries and Grand Marnier; fresh collard greens simmered in red wine, garlic, and butter; and maybe a piece of melon instead of a salad. Wonderful with cold white wine.

Breaded Pork Tenderloin in Grand Marnier and Mushrooms

To make your own cutlets is simple. Take a fresh tenderloin of pork, cut pieces about two inches thick, lay them on a cutting board and just flatten them by hitting them hard with the side of a meat cleaver. It's a very old-fashioned feeling—wear a little gingham and you'll love it. Dip the cutlets first into a mixture of one egg beaten up with a couple of spoons of sour cream, then into breadcrumbs flavored with basil, oregano, marjoram, and Parmesan cheese. Then fry them quickly, just till they brown on the outsides, lay them in a baking pan, and cover with sliced fresh mushrooms. Pour the following Grand Marnier sauce over them and bake uncovered in a 400° oven for half an hour to forty-five minutes.

(Pork in Grand Marnier Sauce)

Grand Marnier Sauce: To half a stick of melted butter in a saucepan, add a handful of sliced shallots, a couple of bay leaves, one small chopped onion, half a cup of Grand Marnier, half a cup of white wine, a pint of heavy cream, and salt and white pepper to taste. Blend all the ingredients and let the mixture simmer for about half an hour.

You could bake pork cutlets as well, or broil them; but I think frying lends the most expression to their taste. Once you fry them, the choice of sauce is entirely up to you. You could simply splash a little lemon juice, orange juice, or white wine across them and serve. Or you might lay the fried cutlets in a baking dish and pour heavy cream or even milk over them. When you bake them, the cream will turn into a sauce.

HAM

You can buy ham in many forms. The ham with water added that you see at the supermarket is not worth the time, effort, and money spent on it. No matter how brilliant the sauce, the ham itself will remain bland, watery, and pulpy. There are several kinds of canned hams—the Polish variety is among the best. There are also fresh hams, salted hams, and other types of cured hams: the Virginia ham, so salty it dries you out for a week; and the "Smithfield" ham—delicious, but still too salty for me. (Smithfield ham, I think, is really best when served in tiny portions on crackers and biscuits for an appetizer.) Fresh ham is wonderful fried with potatoes and eggs for breakfast. My Grandma Hazel in Indiana used to make it for us at five or six in the morning.

As with any meat, however, if you are baking a ham you end up with a much better flavor if there is a bone involved. Across the street from me there lives a gentleman who raises pigs; and now and again he slaughters a pig, smokes it, and sells me a ham. Because of what my neighbor feeds his pigs the meat is tender and juicy; I would say it's the best ham I've ever eaten. Not long ago I bought a twenty-two pound ham and over the course of a few weeks I ate the entire thing myself—with eggs, without eggs, in a little sauce, with greens, with fried peaches, with plums, cold... I don't suggest to anyone that he eat twenty-two pounds of ham by himself, but I do suggest that if you are going out to buy a ham, go to a butcher and make sure you get a smoked ham without water added. (Don't let the butcher tell you they add water to all hams—that's baloney.) Remember, a smoked ham is already cooked, so if you take it home don't feel as though it's got to sit in the oven for six hours. If the ham is fresh, by all means cook it long and slow. If the ham is smoked, here is a lovely way to serve it on a really special occasion.

Ham in Raspberries and Grand Marnier

Score the fatty part of the ham. This means making long cuts through the fat, first in one direction, then again crisscrossing the cuts you've made to make a diamond pattern. It is traditional to shove a whole clove into each of the diamond pieces of fat; lovely but certainly not necessary. You might, in fact, simply sprinkle powdered cloves across the top of the ham. Anyway, once you've scored the ham just put it into a good-sized pan and cook it in a 400° oven for about an hour, uncovered. While that's cooking prepare the sauce below; at the end of the hour, drain off the ham grease and pour the sauce over the meat. Let it cook another half hour, then slice the ham thin onto a serving platter and pour the raspberry sauce over the top.

Raspberry Grand Marnier Sauce: Into a saucepan put one melted stick of butter, half a cup of any kind of prepared mustard, a dash each of A1 sauce, Worcestershire sauce, ginger, cloves, and cinna-

(Ham in Raspberries and Grand Marnier) mon, one cup of brandy, one small can of frozen orange juice concentrate, one-fourth cup of honey, one cup of Grand Marnier, and three cups of fresh raspberries. Simmer it for about half an hour, then pour it over the ham.

The sauce can be changed with almost endless wonderful combinations. The raspberries could be peaches, apricots, nectarines, strawberries, pineapples, apples, mangoes, persimmons, papayas, or any fruit. The spices may be altered; and the Grand Marnier might be chocolate brandy or straight brandy or Amaretto or Cherry Heering. Each will change the character of the dish entirely. The only thing you need to remember about making a sweet fruit sauce for smoked meat is to be sure and add prepared mustard to the sauce; this cuts the too-sweet taste and brings out the salty taste of the ham.

Bacon, people always say, should be soaked in a little water for a minute or two to keep it from shrinking; but this never seems to work for me. However, I find that if you put a little grease in the frying pan and heat it before you add the bacon, the meat will cook more evenly and be juicier. The thick-sliced bacon is preferable because it can be treated more as a meat. I always season bacon: salt, pepper, and a little garlic or basil or marjoram—maybe even the juice of one lemon or a splash of wine or sherry just before I'm ready to take it out of the pan. Try to experiment with as many different things as possible and you'll find that bacon is no longer just a breakfast food but perfect for all kinds of meals. You can make bacon kouffle, whipped-cream pastry with a bacon stuffing and cream gravy on top, a bacon soup, or crepes stuffed with bacon and oysters.

RABBIT

Rabbit is usually bought frozen, though if you live out of the city you'll be able to find fresh rabbit by looking in the classified sections of small newspapers—there is always someone who has rabbits to sell for eating. I once found an ad for peacocks in the local paper. I immediately thought, "What a wonderful idea! I'll serve peacock in a sauce of oranges and brandy and saffron and cream." So I called the fellow up and said, "How big are the peacocks?" He replied that they were about five to six pounds apiece, so I asked him, "How much meat do you think is on 'em?" "Meat!" he cried. "Meat? Whatdaya mean, meat?" "Well," I replied, trying to be as casual as a cook can be, "how many people do you think I could serve on one of them?" "You mean you want to eat them?" he asked. "Not my goddamn peacocks you're not gonna—no sir!" And he slammed down the receiver.

Rabbit is really a wonderful dish. Shake it in flour and fry it in butter with salt and pepper, as you would with chicken. The meat is very white; rabbits eat fresh greens, not garbage. It is also inexpensive and fast-cooking. Start thinking of rabbit as a food, and you will find that it sounds nice with many different sauces, served next to many kinds of dishes.

Rabbit in Red Wine and Pearl Onions, Flamed in Brandy

Put about a cup of flour into a paper bag and generously sprinkle in a good selection of herbs and spices. I use marjoram, thyme, sage, and basil, because they make me think of the woods. Then place your rabbit pieces in the bag and shake it around for a few seconds until you've nicely powdered all the pieces. In a frying pan with about half an inch of melted butter sizzling on the bottom, brown the pieces of rabbit on both sides, seasoning the meat with salt and pepper as it fries. Then

(Rabbit Flambee) remove it from the skillet and place it in a baking pan. To the butter in the frying pan add about a tablespoon of the flour you shook the meat in, and enough peeled, fresh pearl onions to feed the number of people you have. Season the onions with a little sugar, salt, pepper, and thyme and fry them until they begin to turn a little brown. Then slowly add two cups of burgundy, and splash in some soy sauce. Stir it well, beating in a little more flour if the sauce is too thin. Then pour it all over the rabbit, and let it bake at 400°, uncovered, for half an hour. When you take it out of the oven, heat up a cup of brandy, pour it over the rabbit, ignite, and serve. You should be eating this with "Noodles High" (page 133) and collard greens sauteed in champagne—the meal could start with cold cucumber soup and end with homemade watermelon and Creme de Cassis ripple sherbet.

Rabbit is as easy to fix as chicken. Fry it, bake it, and broil it. Boil it with parsnips and make a rabbit broth. I once made a rabbit salad with mayonnaise, chopped celery, chopped onion, and a hard-boiled egg added to cold rabbit pieces. It was really terrific. It was sitting in the refrigerator and my partner Gene Brown came in and made himself a sandwich on black bread. As he was devouring it I asked him how he liked the rabbit salad. "Rabbit? Rabbit? I thought it was a chicken salad," he said as he put the sandwich down. He was ill for two days. I wasn't aware that he couldn't tolerate the thought of eating a rabbit. Guilt, pity, accusation, and even nausea are some of the things to be careful of when serving rabbit. Makes for an interesting evening even when the company is dull.

VENISON

Venison really refers to all game meat, but I usually use it to mean deer meat. You can easily buy frozen venison from New Zealand; it is pretty nice, but not like fresh and wild.

The best way I know of to cook venison comes from an old Shaker recipe. Their suggestion was to make up a flour and water paste, cement the venison roast into that, and bake it for a couple of hours—an intriguing idea.

Canterbury Venison

Make a paste of water and flour, adding green herbs to taste and enough flour so you can roll the paste into a dough. Dry off a six- to eight-pound roast of venison, then rub a little salt, pepper, and sage on it and wrap it tightly in the dough. Bake it at 400° for about two hours. When you break the "cast" off there will be a lot of juice; put it in the blender with a little vegetable extract, a cup of red wine, a dash of hot prepared mustard, a cup of currant jelly or jam, and a little flour to thicken it. Then add a good splash of cognac, put it on the heat until it boils, cut the roast into serving slices, and pour the red wine and currant sauce over the top.

As always, the sauce can be made from whatever you have around. And you can cut the leftover venison into strips, add some sour cream, a little sauerkraut, and some cooked pearl onions, and serve it over wild rice as a "Venison Stroganoff."

Fowl

There is so little fresh fowl, other than chicken and turkey, available today that I often have to travel a hundred miles and more to find fresh quail, mallard duck, partridge, and pheasant. Even if they are frozen, I encourage you to try wild fowl like these, however; if nothing else, it will inspire you to look for fresh. Of course, if there were a market there would be a supply.

Using the more easily available kinds of fowl, I will begin by showing you how you can prepare a dinner for one person, with the breast of a chicken and two vegetables, in about six minutes. I do this really for the single person. Single people should learn to prepare elegant food for themselves; it is all too easy when you are living alone to be careless about eating. The "bother," the "expense," the "difficulty," the lack of an appreciative audience —the excuses are endless and *almost* valid. Consider, however, some of the reasons for cooking fresh food for yourself. First, it's cheaper. Instead of buying a box of frozen something, or a frozen dinner, or lunch meat and bread—the worst thing in the world you could shove into your body—it's cheaper to buy one zucchini, one peach, and one chicken breast. With these three purchases, I will show you how to cook a lovely meal for yourself in minutes.

One of the reasons that single people should take terrific care of themselves (and the best place to start is with eating) is because by and large our society has nothing for the single person. Everything is geared either to meet someone, or to accommodate couples and families. In fact, our society actually makes it difficult for you to be single. Single people pay more taxes, and yet it's not their children who are sucking up the resources in a most disagreeable educational system. For the most part, insurance rates are higher for the single person, the logic being, of course, that he or she is more careless, despondent, and given to suicide, and that single people die young. (Well, it was the insurance companies that made that up, not me.) Also fewer single people collect AFDC or welfare, or buy food stamps. In fact, the single person really carries the brunt of the load; after all, don't electricity, gas, mortgage payments, medical expenses, bread, milk, and meat cost as much for the single person as they do for families? And yet, it's the single person who takes the least of all from the system. Single people, arise! And I don't mean unmarried kids of eighteen and nineteen. I'm talking about people of all ages who are single whether through conditions, sexual preference, choice, or circumstance. So when I tell you you'd better start taking care of yourself, start with this:

Five-Minute Breast of Chicken in a Sour Cream Sauce with Fried Peaches and Zucchini

Melt enough butter to cover the bottom of a frying pan and heat it until it begins to simmer. Flatten a boned chicken breast with the side of a cleaver, or something flat and heavy, and lay it in the simmering butter. Salt and pepper the breast and sprinkle it with thyme. Slice the zucchini into long quarters, lay them in the pan, and sprinkle with salt, pepper, and basil. Then cut a peach in half, remove the pit, and lay the two halves in the simmering butter. Sprinkle with salt, pepper, cinnamon, and sugar;

(Five-Minute Breast of Chicken)

and cook everything over a medium-high flame for about two minutes on each side, spicing the peaches, zucchini, and chicken again after they have been turned. As soon as the chicken is done, remove it and lay it on the dinner plate, then surround it with the zucchini and peaches. Sprinkle about a handful of flour into the frying pan with the greases and drippings, turn the fire to a moderate heat, and stir the flour until it takes up the juices and becomes pasty. Then add a splash of white wine, half a pint of sour cream, and some salt and pepper. Stir until the sauce gets hot, then pour it over the chicken and you're ready to eat.

The entire effort should not take longer than five minutes; and you are preparing a complete dinner with whole, fresh foods using less time and energy than if you were eating frozen, instant, or pre-prepared foods cooked in a microwave oven. You can do the same thing using fish or ham or beef...or you could do it with scrambled eggs...or sprinkle cheese or chives in the sauce and maybe use a little dry sherry or brandy instead of white wine. You could concoct all kinds of private and wonderful dinners for yourself, to enjoy a little of the good life that a lot of other people are missing.

Chicken is truly a wonderful bird; not only does it give us eggs to use in cakes and custards and sauces and ice cream, but the chicken itself can be prepared in so many ways. Some people make a batter of beer and flour and eggs and baking powder, dip the chicken in the batter, and fry it in deep fat or in a skillet with bacon grease. My mother always shook her chicken in seasoned flour, then browned it quickly in a skillet; when it was browned on both sides she would cover it, turn the heat down, and cook it another forty minutes or so, turning it now and again. That's still how I fry chicken today: I think it's the best-tasting fried chicken

I've ever eaten. When you remove the chicken from the pan, add a tablespoon or so of flour to the drippings, stir it until it's as smooth as possible, and then slowly add a cup and a half of milk and a little salt and pepper—a cream gravy to end all cream gravies.

Once I stuffed a five-pound chicken with apples and eggs and sour cream and breadcrumbs and spices, and roasted it in an old cast-iron cook stove. Cook it uncovered for the first half hour, covered for the next half hour; then baste it with about two cups of dry white wine, and let it cook another twenty minutes or so, basting often. Mix a little flour and white wine and sour cream into the drippings, then add the yolks of two eggs and cook it for ten minutes, and you have a wonderful sauce to go with it. It was a lovely evening with two lovely people who are now divorced. And everything is still lovely. Isn't that lovely?

Chicken Breast Stuffed with Prosciutto in Red Wine and Tomatoes

Lay boned chicken breasts on a flat surface. Then lay a slice of prosciutto ham on each one, sprinkle with parsley and a little thyme, and roll them closed. Put them in a baking pan and sprinkle with salt, pepper, paprika, and thyme. Cover and bake in a 400° oven for about thirty minutes. Then uncover and drain the juices into the sauce. Blend the sauce, pour it over the meat, and bake uncovered for another fifteen minutes. Serve.

Sauce: In the blender mix up three whole tomatoes, one cup of red wine, half a cup of melted butter, two tablespoons of flour, three or four shallots, a tablespoon of moist chicken base, the juice of one lemon, some black pepper, marjoram, and a little salt to taste. Place in a saucepan, add one cup of chopped mushrooms, and let simmer for at least half an hour. Pour over chicken breasts.

DUCK

If you can, have the duck split in half right up the middle. Stuffed duck is pleasant but splitting the duck, figuring half per person, will make it so much easier to serve and cut when it comes to eating it. You should lift it off the bottom of the pan on a rack if you can, because duck is so fatty that unless you drain it off in some way the meat will taste greasy.

Roast Duck Blue Strawbery

Preheat the oven to at least 450°, and rub the duck down with a little soy or Worcestershire sauce, some salt and pepper, sage, and ginger. Lay the pieces of duck in the baking pan and bake uncovered for about forty-five minutes. Drain off the grease, pour sauce over the duck, and return it to the oven for another half hour, basting as often as you can remember. This will give the duck a crusty finish as though it's been barbecued.

The obvious sauce for duck has always been orange sauce, though there are classic cherry sauces as well. Experimenting with sauces for duck has always provided good times for me; there are so many sauces you never would imagine that could go on duck. The best combination is usually a sweet one with fruit: one of my favorites is apricots with Amaretto and almonds.

Roast Duck with Apricots, Amaretto, and Almonds

Have your duck split as I suggested and cook it as I explained above. Melt a stick of butter in the bottom of a saucepan and add four thin-sliced shallots, a couple of tablespoons of yellow mustard, the juice of one lemon, half a small can of frozen orange juice concentrate, two cups of washed and pitted fresh apricots, a little salt, and white pepper to taste. Then add one cup of Amaretto liqueur and let the sauce simmer for about forty-five minutes, stirring it

often. Add another cup of Amaretto and a good **(Roast Duck)**
handful of slivered almonds, and you are ready to
ladle it over the duck. Baste the duck with the sauce
as often as possible. You might need a little more of
the liqueur so you can have enough to feel free with
it.

There are other wonderful combinations of fruit and liqueur
for duck sauces: oranges and chocolate brandy; papaya and
whiskey; plums and brandy; plums and Drambuie; damson
plums, mangoes, and champagne. . .or try champagne and sour
cream and sauerkraut, or pimientos and white wine. Just by
changing two ingredients you can create an entirely new and
delicious sauce.

Mallard Duck, on the other hand, is cooked very quickly;
and there is so little fat on a mallard duck it's always wise to put a
little salt pork or bacon on it as you're cooking it.

Spice the mallard duck halves inside and out with a **Mallard Duck**
little salt and pepper and butter, and maybe a little **Flambee**
nutmeg, ginger, allspice, or cinnamon, depending
on what kind of sauce you want to put on the bird.
Wrap mallard halves in bacon and cook them in a
hot oven, about 450°, until the bacon begins to get
crisp and the duck is browned on the top. After it's
cooked, I often take it out of the baking pan and put
it into a skillet on top of the stove, pour the sauce
over the top, and simmer on a low heat, basting
often with the sauce. Just before you serve it, add a
little brandy and light it with a match. Stand back
and try not to wear anything chiffon. (Warm the
brandy in a saucepan before you pour it over
something to be served flaming; it's the only sure-
fire way for it to light.)

TURKEY

One turkey can feed a small family for a week; there is no end to the things you can do with the turkey, whether in the stuffing and roasting, or in the clever use of leftovers. I never buy a frozen turkey, even if I have to travel twenty miles to get one fresh-killed. One bite of the meat of a fresh turkey should convince you for the rest of your life. Almost any butcher will be able to procure a fresh turkey for you.

Roast Stuffed Turkey

To cook a turkey, first you'll need a stuffing. You can buy a prepared bread stuffing but that seems like paying a lot of money for something you always have around the house anyway. My grandmother used to save all the old bread for a week before she made the stuffing—leftover sweet rolls, biscuits, whole wheat, raisin, or rye bread—and toast it all in the broiler. And that's what I do. After you've toasted as much bread as you think you'll need to stuff the turkey, rip it into small pieces and place it in a large mixing bowl. Then for about a twenty- to thirty-pound turkey add about half a pound of melted butter, a couple of pounds of fresh pork sausage, the chopped giblets from the bird, chopped celery and onions, half a bottle of dry white wine, two pints of sour cream, four eggs, a couple of tablespoons of moist chicken base, and salt and white pepper to taste. Stir in two pints of raw oysters with their liquor, plenty of thyme, marjoram, garlic, and basil, and a couple of bay leaves. Then begin to mush it around with your clean hands. That's really the best way to get it done. Squeeze it and mush it till the entire dressing is well fused. If it doesn't look as though you have enough dressing just add more of anything you choose; and if it looks as though you have too much you can bake it in a separate pan and freeze it until some other time.

Fill the two cavities of the bird with the stuffing and close them as best you can. You can tie the openings closed, or sew them shut, or fasten them shut. It's very quick to take a needle and thread and sew it closed—doesn't have to be a lovely stitch, you're going to eat it not wear it. Then rub the whole bird down with a mixture of melted butter, a couple of shots of A1 sauce, some garlic, thyme, and marjoram, and a little red wine. Salt and pepper it well, and place it in a large roasting pan. Then put it into a very hot oven (525°) and bake uncovered for about forty-five minutes. This will singe all the juices into the bird.

Next, take the turkey out of the oven and pour red wine over it until it's well doused. Soak a tea towel (or any piece of cotton that's not terrycloth) in the red wine as well, and when it is soaking wet lay it over the turkey, covering the bird as well as you can. Hit the top with a little more red wine, then cover it all as tightly as you can—I usually seal it with a large sheet of tin foil to make the roasting pan airtight. Turn the oven down to 450°, put the turkey back in, and let it cook for an hour and a half. Then turn the oven off and let it sit all night. Don't open the oven door until the next morning.

When you open the oven door, take the towel off the bird and ladle the juices over the turkey. Then heat it up for about an hour, covered, in a 400° oven.

Here is how to make the best possible gravy with the juices, after removing the turkey to a serving platter: Skim off as much grease as you can, pour

(Roast Stuffed Turkey)

(Roast Stuffed Turkey)

part of the juices into a blender, blend it with a little flour for thickening, and return the mixture to the pan. Heat it until it simmers, adding salt and pepper or whatever you think it might need—maybe a little more red wine, or some sour cream, or heavy cream, or even milk, to stretch the gravy out enough to last you the week. And that's the turkey!

Cooking the bird this way, in its own juices and its own heat, will produce for you the best-tasting, juiciest turkey you've ever eaten. I cooked a thirty-pound bird this way last Thanksgiving using less than three hours worth of energy. You couldn't do that with a microwave oven. And what's even nicer is that you don't have to spend the whole day dealing with the turkey. It's already done, basted, taken care of while you're sleeping.

Besides the usual—turkey croquettes, turkey patties, turkey soups, salads, and pies—there are still many new and terrific ways to serve leftover turkey. It behooves you to try as many new ideas as you can think of, because as lovely as it is, a lot of turkey for a long time can become awfully dull. Here are two fine ways to fix turkey leftovers.

Gravied Turkey over Four-Minute Dumplings

Simply mix any leftover gravy you have with a pint of sour cream, mix in the turkey leftovers, and bring it to a simmer. Serve it over four-minute dumplings. To make the dumplings, mix two eggs, three-quarters of a cup of milk, two cups of flour, and six teaspoons of baking powder. Add salt and any seasoning—with turkey it's nice to use thyme. Bring about one and a half inches of buttered water to a boil in a frying pan that has a lid. Drop in spoonfuls of the batter, cover, cook two minutes, turn them over, cover, and cook another two minutes and they're done. Put the dumplings on a serving platter, ladle the turkey and sauce over them, and serve.

These can be used as an appetizer or an entree. Wash and trim the thick stems from the collards. Fill each leaf with chopped turkey leftovers and roll it up, sticking it with a toothpick to keep the stuffing from falling out. Then make a broth as follows.

Broth: In a large frying pan mix a quart of tomato juice, two cups of white wine, one onion chopped fine, a chopped green pepper, a handful of dill, some hot sauce, the juice of a lemon, white pepper, a dash each of sage and summer savory, and some chicken base. Wash and slice in a pound of fresh mushrooms and a bunch of leeks. Also add any leftover gravy you might have. Bring the mixture to a boil, then turn it down to simmer and place the stuffed collards in the pan. Let them simmer in the broth for half an hour. Serve hot or chilled.

Collard Greens Stuffed with Turkey

GAME BIRDS

The pheasant may be cut in halves or cooked whole; it really doesn't matter since you will be taking it off the bones anyway. Lay a little bacon over the pheasant, salt it, pepper it, and add an herb or spice of your choosing. Bake it, uncovered, at about 475° for about twenty minutes. Remove the pheasant and when it cools enough to handle, take the meat off the bones. (Don't panic thinking you'll need a boning knife and all kinds of expertise: this can all be done by hand.) Put all the skin and bones into a good-sized pot, and lay the meat itself in a baking dish and put it to the side.

In the blender mix one stick of melted butter, a small onion, two tomatoes, the juice of one orange,

Boned Pheasant in a Cognac Game Sauce

(Pheasant in Cognac Game Sauce)

two cups of white wine, a couple of bay leaves, some thyme, marjoram, garlic, and pepper, a spoon or so of chicken base, a couple of mushrooms, some summer savory and sweet basil, and maybe a couple of tablespoons of flour just to thicken the sauce. Blend it all until smooth and place it in the saucepan with the bones. Add plenty of sliced mushrooms, and let the sauce simmer for at least an hour. Then add a cup of heavy cream, half a cup of cognac, and salt and pepper to taste. Pour the sauce and mushrooms over the pheasant in the baking dish and cook it uncovered in a 400° oven for forty to forty-five minutes. Serve right from the baking dish. A wonderful entree—served with wild rice flavored with oranges, a fresh green vegetable, and a bottle of red wine, it would make a memorable dinner.

Of course, the only process to concern yourself with is the cooking of the pheasant. Once you get that down, the sauce can be whatever you'd like it to be. You simply boil the bones and skin down and add a collection of anything you'd like. You could use red wine, sherry, or even whiskey in the sauce; or leave the cognac out altogether and use Cointreau, which will give the sauce a slightly orange flavor that is wonderful on pheasant. On pages 99 to 105 there are some ideas for sauces that may be used on just about everything.

Pheasant Stuffed with Artichoke Hearts in a Champagne Sauce

As posh as this might sound, it really is not that financially out of reach. If you must, use two cans of artichoke hearts; if you use fresh artichokes you'll need about a dozen and a half. Place the hearts in a bowl and add one melted stick of butter, one small chopped onion, a stalk of fine-chopped celery, two eggs, the juice of one lemon, about half a pound of fresh pork sausage, a couple of spoons of moist chicken base, some white pepper and salt to taste, a little allspice, one cup of champagne, and enough flavored breadcrumbs to hold it all together. Stuff the cavities of the bird and close them tightly. Sprinkle the bird with salt, pepper, and thyme, and lay a few strips of bacon over the top. Cook uncovered in a 475° oven for fifteen minutes, then turn it down to 400°, pour the rest of the bottle of champagne over the bird, and let it cook for another forty-five minutes. Remove the pheasant and set it onto a serving platter. Pour the remaining juices from the pan into a blender with a tablespoon of flour, two eggs, and salt and pepper to taste; blend until smooth. Return the sauce to the heat for another few minutes, until it begins to thicken up from the eggs and flour; then pour it into a dish and ladle it over the pheasant after it has been served.

(Pheasant Stuffed with Artichokes in Champagne)

The thing to remember about pheasant is how easy it is to cook; once you put it in the oven it just about cooks itself. The stuffing and sauce can change every time, making the bird an entirely different kind of dish each time you do it. You can stuff it with oysters or crabmeat, fruit or vegetables, pork sausage or veal; the sauce might be made with sparkling burgundy, sour cream, sweet cream, red wine, white wine, sherry, or vodka—or a combination of several things. If the pheasant was shot be sure to keep an eye open for the buckshot—pick it all out if you can. When the bird is boned it's very easy to find the buckshot, but if you leave it whole you'll want to take special care so your guest doesn't put a five-hundred-dollar crown down on a hunk of pellet. There could be serious ramifications.

Cornish Game Hens are wonderful little birds—so dependable, so good. They are only one step away from being tiny chickens, but there is a lot of meat on one—so much that you can cut them in half and serve half a hen to each person. Since you can rarely buy them fresh you'll have to settle for frozen; have the butcher saw them down the center while they are still frozen to save you the trouble of doing it yourself. Cornish hens are unbelievably simple to cook, and they are relatively inexpensive, which allows you to splurge a little on the ingredients for the sauce.

Cornish Hens in a Lobster and Sour Cream Sauce

Preheat the oven to 475°. Split the hens down the center, and season inside and out with salt, pepper, paprika, and thyme. Then lay them in the baking pan and cook uncovered in the oven for about thirty minutes. Remove them, splash white wine across them, cover them, and place them back in the oven for another half hour. Remove them, lay them on a serving platter, pour a sauce over, and serve.

Lobster and Sour Cream Sauce: Melt a stick of butter in the bottom of a saucepan. Add half a dozen sliced shallots, a tablespoon or so of moist chicken base, and a little flour for thickening. Stir in half a cup of dry sherry, half a cup of white wine, one pint of sour cream, half a pint of heavy cream, some white pepper and tarragon, and the juice of one lemon. Let the sauce simmer for about three-quarters of an hour and then run it through the blender with one whole egg. Add salt and pepper if needed, place it back in the saucepan, and add a pound of shelled lobster meat. (Lobster body meat costs only about half what tails and claws, out of the shell, might cost, and it tastes terrific. I wouldn't suggest it unless I had tried it myself and been pleased.) Just mix the lobster into the hot sauce, pour it over the hens, and serve. It's a very elegant dish. I've also done this sauce using heavy cream, champagne, and crabmeat.

It must be obvious by now how you go about working the sauces around to suit your particular tastes or to work with what you happen to have on hand. There are always only two or three main ingredients in every sauce; once you learn to add your own favorite ingredients you will be cooking brilliantly without recipes.

Cornish Hens Wrapped in Ham in a Sour Cream and Sherry Sauce

Split the hens in half and rub them inside and out with salt, pepper, and thyme. Wrap a slice of ham around each one, and place in a baking pan. Bake covered in a 400° oven for thirty minutes. Uncover, drain off juices into sauce, blend the sauce, and pour it back over the hens. Cook them uncovered for another twenty minutes and serve.

Sauce: Melt half a stick of butter with two tablespoons of flour for thickening, three or four shallots sliced thin, half a cup of cream sherry, a pint of sour cream, two tablespoons of chicken base, paprika, thyme, white pepper, and salt to taste.

Quail is another bird you can almost never get fresh, if you can get it at all. They are tiny little birds, and should be baked or cooked in a sauce quickly so they don't become tough. You should plan on two per person at least, although there is more meat on these little birds than you would imagine. If you do plan to serve only one per person, it would be a good idea to stuff them with something special like lobster tails or crabmeat. You'll be astonished at how far a tiny quail will go when stuffed with a filling meat.

Quail makes a lovely breakfast, brunch, dinner, or late supper. Pretty elegant eating for breakfast or brunch, but certainly there might be at least one occasion when you'd like to have a quail for breakfast. In that event, here is a pleasant way to serve it.

Breakfast Quail

If you were serving four people quail for breakfast you would need eight quail, washed and buttered inside and out. Then prepare a stuffing: mix two eggs, half a cup of chablis, a shot of apricot brandy, some salt and pepper, a dash of mustard and of cardamom, and a good handful of breadcrumbs. Mix in two pounds of pitted apricots, and mash the ingredients together well.

Pack the stuffing into the birds, wrap them in bacon slices, and cook them in a baking dish, uncovered, at 450° for about ten minutes. While they are cooking mix up half a cup of frozen orange juice concentrate, a quarter cup of melted butter, a splash of champagne, a dash of Worcestershire sauce, a spoonful of prepared mustard, and salt and pepper to taste. After the birds have been cooking for ten minutes, drain off the bacon grease and pour over the orange and champagne sauce. Place the pan back in the oven and let the birds cook for another twenty minutes, basting often with the sauce.

Quail are very easy to cook simply because they are small and take no time at all. They have very little fat; you can wrap bacon or salt pork around them to keep them moist. The sauces and stuffings you can make for quail are many and varied. Crab or lobster stuffing is done in a simple way: as much crabmeat or lobster as you'll need, mixed with melted butter, fine-chopped mushrooms, breadcrumbs, an egg to bind it together, a little moist chicken base to give it some depth, white pepper, and a little tarragon or chervil. Or stuff them with plums, peaches, nectarines, raspberries, or strawberries. Just remember that you want to avoid the stuffing being too sweet—this is easily accomplished by adding a dash of mustard to the stuffing.

Partridge, also, is hard to find fresh, unless of course you or a friend have managed to shoot one or two yourself. They are lovely when roasted in an oyster sauce.

Partridge Roasted in Sherry and Oysters

Cut the partridge in halves the long way, from the neck to the tail. Rub them inside and out with melted butter, salt, white pepper, and thyme. Sprinkle the tops with paprika, lay a couple of rashers of bacon on each one, and bake uncovered in a 425° oven for twenty minutes. Then take them out, drain off the bacon grease, and pour the following sauce over. Cover and bake at 400° for another twenty minutes in the sauce. Remove from the oven and serve immediately.

Oyster Sauce: In a saucepan melt half a stick of butter, then slice in about six shallots and let them simmer until they have turned brown. (Try not to burn the butter.) Add a couple of spoonfuls of flour to thicken, and stir the mixture into a thick paste. Then add half a cup of a dry white wine, and the liquor from two pints of fresh oysters. Stir until smooth, and add a cup of tomato juice, half a cup of dry sherry, one chopped tomato, the juice of one lime, a dash of tabasco sauce, some tarragon, and white pepper. Let the sauce simmer for about half an hour, and just before you pour it over the partridge add the two pints of oysters. Stir them into the sauce well, pour it all over the birds, cover, and let cook.

Merely by using crabmeat instead of oysters—or langostinos, lobster, clams, or crayfish—the sauce will be different and brilliant each time. The other ingredients can just as easily be worked about. Use all white wine instead of mixing it with sherry, or leave out the tomato juice and use chicken stock, or change the oysters to apples, leaving the rest of the ingredients as they are — and you will have a completely different sauce.

The partridge itself, like all meats and fish and fowl, is very simple to cook. It's the sauces that are different, and they are almost as easy as the main ingredient. Remember, before you give up on any original combination that you don't think is going to work, add a little more salt and a little white wine and let it cook another half hour.

Fish

When I was growing up in Chicago, there were just two kinds of fish that poor Catholics ever ate: frozen halibut and tuna casserole. I never cook halibut now, but tuna comes to me in the form of a salad now and again. Tuna salad can be delicious: chop hard-boiled eggs, celery, and onions into it, and use a little vinegar and oil (instead of mayonnaise) with a lot of salt and pepper. Fresh tuna fried in vinegar and butter will simply astound you. Just salt and pepper the fresh tuna, fry it in a pan of sizzling butter for a couple of minutes on each side, then splash some vinegar into the butter before you take the fish from the pan. Use a little garlic also and lemon or lime juice. If you've never eaten fresh tuna go down to the fish market sometime and demand that they stock it. It's a lot cheaper fresh than it is by can. And you can still turn it into a tuna casserole, God forbid.

Just about all fish should be cooked as quickly as possible, as though you were bringing it just past the point of being glassy. Also, soaking fish in lime juice will cook it. (I learned that from the Japanese.) And, like the Japanese, if you can acquire a taste for raw fish you are most fortunate. Raw fish with a little lime juice gives you about as much natural taste of the fish as you'll ever find.

There is an endless variety of fish to work with—cod, salmon, swordfish, sturgeon, shark, fillet of sole, red snapper, lobster, frogs' legs, squid, shrimp, eel—but I would like to share some of my favorite fish and the way that I've done them, so that you'll get an idea of how it's done and be able to launch into incredible fish dishes of your own: fish sauces, fish stuffings, and fish soups large and well-stocked enough to be a main course.

I don't cook any piece of fish longer than fifteen minutes, and usually it's about twelve minutes, six on either side. All fish can be excellently prepared in just a matter of minutes. Fillets, dipped in flour and fried in butter with a little salt and pepper and lemon juice, are wonderful, especially fresh trout—speckled, rainbow, or freshwater. Any whole fish can be stuffed and baked within twenty minutes. Probably the only thing wrong you can do to a fish is to overcook it.

Striped Bass in a Crabmeat and Shrimp Sauce

Lay the bass fillet in a buttered baking pan and sprinkle with salt, pepper, lime juice, and tarragon. Bake uncovered in a 400° oven for about eight minutes. Then drain the juices off into the sauce and pour it over the fish. Return it to the oven for another eight minutes and serve.

Sauce: Mix melted butter, shallots, one cup of chablis, one cup of tomato juice, a splash of dry sherry, the juice of one lemon, the juices from the baked fish, and salt and white pepper to taste. Let simmer for half an hour, then add one cup each of crabmeat and raw shrimp.

Have the fish market cut your swordfish steaks
about three-quarters of an inch thick. Cook the
sauce before you take the fish from the refrigerator,
then cut the fish into the size pieces you prefer.
Swordfish can be two feet wide at times; if that's the
case you could easily feed six people with one cut.
Cover the bottom of a saucepan with melted butter
—probably about three-quarters of a stick; a little
less or more will not ruin the outcome. Then slice a
couple of shallots into the butter, add a couple of
tablespoons of flour for thickening, stir it into a
good paste, and add one cup of white wine. Stir that
well so the sauce will be smooth without your having
to run it through the blender. Then add a splash of
dry sherry, a cup of light cream, and a cup of sour
cream. Season with salt and white pepper to taste.
Then add the juice of one lime and a tablespoon of
tarragon, and let the sauce simmer for about half an
hour, stirring every few minutes so that it doesn't
separate or stick to the bottom of the pan.

Put a little butter in the bottom of a baking dish,
lay in the fish, sprinkle a little lemon juice, salt, and
pepper over it, and place it in a 450° oven for about
eight minutes. Take it out of the oven and drain the
juice into the sauce. Add a shot of coffee brandy,
stir the sauce well, then pour it all over the fish and
return it to the oven for another five to eight minutes. You might sprinkle it with a little tarragon and
paprika before you put it back into the oven but it's
not necessary. It's a lovely sauce that can be used on
fish, fowl, or meat. The only impetus you need is a
little nerve.

Swordfish in Coffee Brandy and Sour Cream

When I say "to taste," which I do often in this book, I expect that you will in fact add the salt and pepper, or whatever, to your taste — to your liking. Don't skimp on seasoning. You can go to any chain restaurant in the world and taste dull, bland, boring cooking. Those cooks are taught to cook that way. They are told that "the customer likes to add his own seasoning," which of course turns out to be only salt and pepper. Everyone who eats in a chain restaurant does add salt and pepper before he even tastes the food, because that's all there is sitting around to season the food with, except maybe mustard or catsup.

Salmon in a Sauce Marguerite

In a saucepan mix the following: two cups of Blue Strawbery Party Cheese (see page 41), one tablespoon of moist chicken base, a cup of dry white wine, a splash of dry sherry, a splash of white vermouth, half a stick of butter, the juice of one lime, a dash of flour for thickening, two cups of heavy cream, a few shallots, and salt and white pepper to taste. Simmer the ingredients for about twenty minutes or half an hour, and then blend the mixture until smooth.

Lay the salmon fillets in a buttered baking dish, sprinkle with lemon juice and tarragon, pour the hot sauce over the fish, and bake uncovered in a preheated 450° oven for about twelve minutes. Serve.

You could do this dish exactly as I have, or change around whatever you like. You might make the dish with the sauce, then cover it and let it sit overnight in the refrigerator and serve it cold for breakfast, brunch, lunch, or whatever. Fresh salmon is very flexible. The point of all this is to stress the simplicity of cooking a fine salmon: twelve minutes in a 450° oven, and if the salmon is just large enough for two servings I would watch the time even more closely. I recently cooked a ten-pound salmon, stuffed with peas and mushrooms and wrapped in tin foil, on an open pit. The whole procedure took me about twenty minutes, and the fish was done to perfection. The sauce, like all the sauces in this book, is entirely up to you—whatever you think might be lovely on a salmon: tomatoes and Grand Marnier, sherry and lemon egg sauce, grapefruit and almonds. A chilled salmon dish with sauce is also perfect for an appetizer (see page 25).

Stuffing fillets and whole fish is a relatively easy proposition. The stuffing for a fish must be partially cooked ahead of time because the fish bakes for such a short time. The salmon mentioned above was stuffed with a mixture of cooked fresh peas, two eggs, a couple of cups of fried mushrooms, one very small onion, a dash of chicken base, some salt and pepper, a little sweet basil, and some breadcrumbs, along with a melted stick of butter. I packed the cavity of the fish with the stuffing, rubbed the fish down with some melted butter, lemon juice, and tarragon, salted and peppered it, then wrapped it in double-strength foil and placed it on an open barbecue grill. After about ten minutes on one side I turned it over and did another ten minutes on the other side. I served it with Sauce Marguerite. Once again, the fish can be served hot or cold. It could also be baked indoors in a baking dish or one of those clay roasting dishes. In that case, keep the salmon covered, but do not try to turn it. It will cook easily on both sides in the oven.

Any size fish can be stuffed. I am, of course, not referring to bullheads although I imagine they could be amazing with a stuffing of pimientos and oranges. I am thinking instead of red snapper, trout, bluefish, mackerel. They might be stuffed with fruit, breadcrumbs, rice, other fish, vegetables. I continually try to explore the different possibilities for stuffing fish—or cooking anything for that matter. Remember, the basics for almost every stuffing for fish are melted butter, a couple of eggs for binding, some breadcrumbs to hold it all together, and anything else you want to add, including the spices. Sherry, white wine, white vermouth, rose, or even a little red wine can make the stuffing an elegant and complete dish. For instance:

Crabmeat Stuffing for Fillet of Sole

Combine half a stick of melted butter, a pound of fresh crabmeat, one egg, half a cup of breadcrumbs, a dash of garlic, a dash of Parmesan cheese, dashes of white pepper, oregano, and basil, and a splash of dry sherry. If the mixture is too thin add more crabmeat or breadcrumbs. Lay a generous spoonful onto a fillet of sole, wrap the ends around, and stick it with a toothpick to hold it together. Place it in a buttered baking dish and bake uncovered in a preheated 450° oven for about twelve minutes. Then mix up and pour across the top one melted stick of butter, the juice of one lemon, a dash of garlic, white pepper and salt, and a splash of white wine.

Instead of crabmeat, Parmesan cheese, dry sherry, and the spices I suggested for a stuffing, you might try the same amounts of chopped grapefruit, slivered almonds, white wine, tarragon, and cardamom. The sauce could remain the same, or you can leave out the garlic and blend the butter and wine into two egg yolks, return to the heat, cook for a couple of minutes on a low flame, and then blend again. It becomes almost a hollandaise but with a taste of your own. Add whatever spice or herb you prefer.

Or you might stuff a fish with this very simple, inexpensive, and delicious stuffing: Start again with melted butter and egg, adding one cup of breadcrumbs or prepared stuffing, a little Parmesan cheese, some garlic and lemon juice, a little sherry or wine, salt and pepper to taste, and a couple of stalks of fresh celery chopped fine. This basic stuffing can be made more involved by adding a cup of cooked mushrooms, crabmeat, lobster meat, cooked oysters or clams, or chopped snails. The possibilities are endless.

Lobsters can be boiled very simply thus: Bring a large pot of salted water to a boil and plunge the lobster into it head first, so that you can't hear it scream. Let it cook for about fifteen minutes. If you plan to use the meat in another dish, cook it only until the shell turns orange. Lobster meat can be tough if it's overcooked, and at the price you pay for it you certainly don't want to make a failure. It's best to break the body shell over the sink to get rid of the excess water picked up in the boiling. Then remove the meat and it is ready — either to eat with melted butter and lemon juice or to use in casseroles, coquilles, or stuffing. Here's a delicious way to use lobster meat:

Avocado Stuffed with Lobster Meat

Peel and halve as many avocados as you'll need for the number of people you are serving. Make certain they are ripe — not mushy, but soft to the touch — as cooking an unripe avocado leaves a bitter taste. Remove the pit and lay the avocado halves on a buttered baking dish. Remove the meat from a cooked lobster (or you might simply buy a pound or so of lobster meat already out of the shell — you really get a lot of meat in a pound). In a saucepan combine a stick of melted butter, a good spoonful of flour for thickening, a couple of sliced shallots, a handful of parsley or chervil, some white pepper, chicken base, paprika, and salt, a shot of dry sherry, a pinch of tarragon, and about a pint of heavy cream. Blend the sauce in the blender with two eggs, then simmer for ten to fifteen minutes, blend again, and mix in the pound of lobster meat. Add the juice of a lemon and about half a cup of breadcrumbs. Fill the avocado halves with the lobster stuffing, keeping about half a cup aside for the sauce. Then bake them uncovered at 400° for ten or fifteen minutes, remove onto a serving platter, and pour the sauce over.

Sauce: Take the half cup of leftover lobster stuf-

(Stuffed Avocado) fing and put it into a blender with the juice of one lemon, half a cup of white wine, a little white pepper, salt, and a half cup of heavy cream. Blend until smooth, put on a medium heat, and let simmer for about fifteen minutes, about as long as the avocados are baking. Puree the sauce again and pour it over the avocados.

Instead of the lemon juice use a shot of kirsch, and add a couple of tablespoons of smoked Edam cheese, grated. The effect is novel and delicious.

Crabmeat is done in almost the same way as lobster meat. If you're dealing with king crabmeat it will more than likely be frozen. Thaw it out slowly, place it in a scallop shell or casserole, pour a sauce over it, and bake it for about twelve minutes. If you are cooking fresh crab, as with lobster drop it into boiling water and let it cook until the shell turns orange. Then pick the meat out and either eat it with melted butter and lemon juice, or turn it into a casserole or stuff something with it. Here is something delicious to make with seafood and chicken breast.

Fisherman's Casserole Mix equal amounts of scallops, chopped squid, raw shrimp, and boned diced chicken breast. Fry them in a melted stick of butter and a tablespoon of olive oil until tender, seasoning with garlic, lemon juice, salt, and pepper. Then remove the meats, saving the juices for sauce, and place in a bowl. Pour the drippings into a blender, add two tablespoons of flour, a cup of white wine, a splash of white vermouth, a little nutmeg and tarragon, and salt and pepper. Blend until smooth, mix it into the fish and chicken, top with breadcrumbs flavored with lemon and butter, and bake uncovered in a 500° oven for about fifteen minutes. This makes a lovely appetizer served in scallop shells.

Sauces

There is no end to the number of sauces you can make for meat, fish, fowl, and vegetables. I have put together here a collection of sauces that I have been successful with at Blue Strawbery. Almost all of them can be worked around and used on more than one entree. Feel loose about them — as with the rest of the suggestions in this book, the measurements needn't be exact; and along with the sauces I will give you suggestions as to what they might be best over.

In a saucepan melt half a stick of butter and bring it to a simmer. Add about five thin-sliced shallots, a couple of beef bouillon cubes, some basil and marjoram, a good spoon each of mustard, catsup, A1 sauce, and Worcestershire sauce, one chopped onion, and a fifth of sparkling burgundy. Let the sauce simmer down and thicken for about an hour. Add three cans of drained artichoke hearts, let simmer another half hour, and ladle over beef.

Sparkling Burgundy and Artichoke Sauce

**Chocolate Brandy
Sour Cream Sauce**

Mix in a saucepan one melted stick of butter, a handful of shallots, and a couple of spoonfuls of flour for thickening. Stir in a pint of sour cream, a tablespoon of chervil, white pepper and salt to taste, half a cup of white wine, and a quarter cup of chocolate brandy. Simmer the mixture for twenty minutes to half an hour, puree it in a blender, and pour over the entree. Using all the same ingredients but changing the liqueur, you might try the sauce with Amaretto, apricot brandy, coffee brandy, cognac, whiskey, Drambuie, or vodka—or with whatever you might have handy. The sauce can be used on all birds from chicken to quail and also on veal and most fish dishes; it will taste different on each of these things.

**Almond and
Swiss Cheese Sauce**

In a saucepan melt half a stick of butter with about two tablespoons of flour for thickening. Make a nice paste out of it and slowly add the following ingredients, stirring often so that the sauce remains smooth and won't need to be blended: two cups of rose wine, one tablespoon of moist chicken base, a few dashes of allspice, white pepper and salt to taste, and half a pound of slivered almonds. Simmer for about thirty minutes, stirring often.

Over whatever entree you might be cooking, for the last fifteen minutes lay a slice of Swiss cheese and then pour over the sauce. Serve in the same dish you bake in. This sauce is good on boned turkey, pheasant, or chicken breasts.

**Cream Cheese, Leeks,
and Whiskey Sauce**

Brown a bunch of washed and chopped leeks in a melted stick of butter. Add a couple of tablespoons of flour for thickening, two eight-ounce packages of cream cheese, half a cup of white wine, about half a cup of grated cheddar cheese, and half a cup of light cream. Season with nutmeg, salt, and pepper to taste; then add two shots of a nice whiskey. Let the sauce simmer for about half an hour, pour over the entree, and serve. Terrific on all birds, tenderloin of beef, and veal.

(Cream Cheese and Whiskey Sauce)

Chop a medium-sized red onion and simmer in half a stick of melted butter until it's soft. Then thicken with two tablespoons of flour, and add two tablespoons of moist chicken base, a cup of amontillado sherry, and a cup and a half of heavy cream. Season to taste with salt, white pepper, and tarragon. Add two cups of sliced mushrooms to the sauce and let simmer for half an hour. Stir often so the sauce doesn't separate. Pour over any bird, veal, or beef dish.

Sherry and Mushroom Cream Sauce

In a blender mix one melted stick of butter, two tablespoons of flour, the juice of one lime, three cups of burgundy, some tarragon, and salt and white pepper to taste. Blend until smooth; then simmer the sauce for forty-five minutes to an hour. Add a cup of crabmeat, and ladle over entree. This sauce is terrific on pheasant, wild turkey, chicken breast, sturgeon, and shark fillets.

Crab and Burgundy Sauce

Melt a stick of butter with three or four sliced shallots, and thicken with two tablespoons of flour. Then add a few dashes of curry powder, salt and white pepper, the juice of one lemon, about a quarter cup of catsup, and a pint of sour cream. Smooth all the ingredients in the blender and simmer for about half an hour on a low flame, then add half a cup of white wine. Pour over the entree

Golden Cream Sauce

(Golden Cream Sauce)

and serve; or let the entree bake in the sauce for about fifteen minutes. This sauce is most desirable on partridge or any other game bird, or with crab and lobster meat.

Sherry Oyster Sauce

Melt half a stick of butter and thicken with two tablespoons of flour. Flavor with a handful of chervil, a tablespoon of chicken base, two cups of dry sherry, and salt and white pepper to taste. Let the sauce simmer for at least forty-five minutes on a low flame, then stir in two pints of raw, shucked oysters with their juice, and let cook another fifteen to twenty minutes. Ladle over the entree. This sauce is good on partridge, pheasant, shark steaks, sturgeon, and swordfish.

Burgundy Sour Cream Sauce

In a blender mix half a stick of melted butter, two tablespoons of flour, a tablespoon of moist chicken base, a handful of parsley, three tomatoes, a pint of sour cream, two cups of burgundy, and salt and white pepper to taste. Simmer in a saucepan for about forty-five minutes before serving. If you cook birds in it, blend the sauce again after the birds are finished. I've used this sauce on wild turkey; it's also good on stuffed chicken breast.

Burgundy Fondue Sauce

In a saucepan slowly bring to a simmer the following: half a stick of butter, two tablespoons of flour, two cups of burgundy, half a pound of Swiss cheese, one pound of sharp white cheddar cheese, a good shot of kirsch, one tablespoon of moist chicken base, and salt and white pepper to taste. Good on all birds, veal, and rabbit.

Mix in a blender half a stick of melted butter, two to three tablespoons of flour for thickening, three cups of burgundy, two tablespoons of moist beef base, a splash each of A1 and Worcestershire sauces, a large pinch of savory, and white pepper to taste. Blend until smooth, pour into a saucepan, and add half a pound of chopped mushrooms and a cup of drained sauerkraut. Let simmer for forty-five minutes to an hour. This sauce is wonderful on wild or domestic turkey, rabbit, and venison.

Sauerkraut, Mushroom, and Burgundy Sauce

In the bottom of a saucepan melt one stick of butter, then add about four shallots, sliced thin, and let them simmer until they are limp and beginning to brown. Then add a couple of tablespoons of prepared mustard, the juice of one lemon, a quarter cup of Worcestershire sauce, two cinnamon sticks, a dash of cardamom, six to eight plums, pitted and cut into the sauce, half a cup of plum preserves, and one cup of brandy. Let the sauce simmer on a low flame for about an hour. Then pour over meat, either to bake in the sauce or to serve immediately. It is very effective on smoked breast of turkey, duck, mallard duck, goose, ham, lamb, and venison.

Plum and Brandy Sauce

In the blender puree one melted stick of butter, two tablespoons of flour, one cup of white wine (liebfraumilch is wonderful, but a drier wine will work as well), a good amount of chervil, and a pint of natural yogurt. Blend until smooth, return to the saucepan, and add three or four sliced unpeeled apples. Cook for about half an hour. If the sauce is too thin from the juice of the apples, ladle a cupful into the blender and add more flour, then return to the sauce. Great served on Cornish hen, mallard duck, or roast chicken.

Yogurt, White Wine, and Apple Sauce

Burgundy, Oyster, and Mushroom Sauce

In the blender mix half a stick of melted butter, three tablespoons of flour for thickening, a tablespoon of catsup, a tablespoon of moist chicken base, a generous pinch of tarragon, half a pint of sour cream, and two cups of burgundy. Blend until smooth; then pour into a saucepan and let simmer for fifteen to twenty minutes. Add half a pound of sliced mushrooms and a pint of fresh, shucked oysters with their juice. Simmer for twenty minutes to half an hour. Delicious ladled over Cornish hen, partridge, turkey, pheasant, chicken, swordfish, sturgeon, or shark.

Champagne, Yogurt, and Apricot Sauce

Melt a stick of butter in the bottom of a saucepan and stir in about three tablespoons of flour so that it makes a paste. Then add a pint of unflavored yogurt, three pitted fresh apricots or a handful of dried, a tablespoon of moist chicken base, white pepper and salt to taste, a generous pinch of chervil, and a split of champagne. (You could also use Cold Duck.) Simmer. May be used on quail, partridge, chicken, pheasant, turkey.

Brandied Sour Cream and Date Sauce

You'll need to do this in two saucepans. In one melt a stick of butter and add one pound of dried dates and a cup of brandy. Simmer until the dates are well saturated but not mushy and soft. In the other pan combine half a cup of dry sherry, a pint of sour cream, and a good pinch of tarragon, with a little flour for thickening. (You might smooth this in the blender to thicken it up a bit.) Let both sauces cook for twenty minutes to half an hour, then combine them and pour over the entree. This sauce is especially nice on duck.

Put into a blender one melted stick of butter, a couple of sliced shallots, about three tablespoons of flour for thickening, some white pepper, a few shakes of cardamom, and a quarter cup of prepared mustard. Blend until smooth, pour into a saucepan, and add a split of champagne (or Cold Duck), one cup of brandy, one cup of white raisins, half a dozen pitted and sliced nectarines, one cup of blueberry preserves, and about half a cup of frozen orange juice concentrate. Simmer the sauce for at least an hour; if it becomes a little dry add more brandy. A nice sauce for any bird, ham, or lamb.

Champagne and Brandy Sauce with Nectarines, Blueberries, and Raisins

Into the blender put half a stick of melted butter, three tablespoons of flour, half a lemon with peelings, three cups of chablis, a good amount of chervil, two tablespoons of moist beef base, and a few shakes of Worcestershire sauce. Blend well, place in a saucepan, and bring to a boil. Turn the heat down and simmer for about half an hour, then add a pound of whole fresh mushrooms. Let the sauce cook for another half hour until the mushrooms are tender, and then pour it over veal, tenderloin of beef, prime rib roast, rabbit, or well done pork.

White Wine, Lemon, and Mushroom Sauce

Vegetables

There is absolutely no end to the incredible things that can be done with vegetables. You could create a delicious six-course dinner consisting only of vegetables without ever repeating any one ingredient, including the spices or wines that you use for cooking. For example, you could begin with Cream of Pumpkin Soup, follow with Fresh Asparagus in a Hollandaise Sauce, Belgian Endive in a Pimiento Mousse, Crepes Stuffed with Curried Sweet Potatoes and Mushrooms in a White Wine and Watercress Cream Sauce, Saffron and Lime Pilaf, Fried Zucchini, and Pearl Onions Flambeed in Brandy, and finish with Carrot Ice Cream. I am not a vegetarian but I've often been served vegetarian meals that were mundane and boring. Deliver me from brown rice—I don't care how much pineapple you put into it. It is even possible to prepare the above dinner without using any animal byproducts—if you are completely vegetarian. My point, of course, is that vegetables do not have to be the low point of a dinner.

I have already said that you should never cook vegetables in water. Cooking any green vegetable with just a little butter, salt, and pepper in a tightly covered container will bring out its own natural taste. If you boil green vegetables in water you simply end up with soft nothing — a little on the green side. Often I fry green vegetables, such as green beans with a couple of slices of bacon; or asparagus in butter, then quickly sauteed with a few drops of white wine; or Brussels sprouts in butter. Have you ever simmered a green vegetable in heavy cream and salt and pepper? On occasion I will season a green vegetable with an herb or spice, but generally I feel that the vegetable by itself carries such a wonderful and distinct flavor of its own that to use anything more than salt and pepper detracts from its taste — except that I always add a little honey to fresh peas. (Honey also adds the "fresh" taste to frozen orange juice. Add a few drops of honey to a can of frozen orange or grapefruit juice or whatever frozen concentrate you might be using. It will taste as though it's fresh-squeezed.)

One of the ways I learn is to take a vegetable and see how many ways I can use it, how many things it can become. Almost all yellow vegetables can be used somehow in every course from the soup to the dessert. Of course you wouldn't want to do it all in the same meal, but the more you know about vegetables and what you can do with them the better prepared you'll be when something unexpected happens — like dropping the dessert on the living room carpet before you've vacuumed.

This course-by-course progression of carrot dishes illustrates my point:

Carrot and Saffron Cream Soup

In a saucepan melt a stick of butter with a couple of tablespoons of flour for thickening and two washed and thin-sliced leeks. Then add two cups of washed, peeled, and diced carrots, one cup of a dry white wine, two cups of heavy cream, two tablespoons of moist chicken base, the outer rind of half an orange (peeled off the top of the orange with a potato peeler), a pinch of saffron, a handful of chopped chives, a quarter cup of orange juice concentrate, salt and white pepper to taste, and the juice of one lemon. Simmer the ingredients for about an hour on a low flame, stirring often. Then run the mixture through the blender again, adding more cream (or white wine) if the soup is too thick, and more flour or the yolks of two eggs if the mixture is too thin.

Crab Legs in a Sherry and Carrot Sauce

Lay king crab legs in a baking dish or small baking shell. (Figure at least two legs per person if you are using this as an appetizer; more if you mean this to be the main course.) Then pour sauce over the crabmeat and bake uncovered in a 400° oven for twelve to fifteen minutes.

The sauce is elementary. In a saucepan melt three-quarters of a stick of butter until it sizzles. Add about four or five thin-sliced shallots, one tablespoon of moist chicken base, a heaping table-spoon of flour for thickening, white pepper to taste, one tablespoon of tarragon, about half a cup of dry sherry, one cup of washed and diced carrots, and one cup of Clamato juice. Simmer at least half an hour, then smooth it in the blender, pour it over the crab legs, and bake in a preheated 400° oven for twelve to fifteen minutes. Remove and serve while still sizzling.

Carrot and Port Wine Sherbet

Peel and dice two cups of carrots. Simmer them in two cups of port wine until soft to the touch of a fork, and then puree it all in a blender. Add half a cup or so of Rose's lime juice, a small can of frozen orange juice concentrate, the juice of two lemons, and enough honey just to take the edge off the tart-ness (half a cup to a cup). Mix until perfectly smooth, then pour into ice-cube trays and place them in the freezer. When it begins to harden around the edges take it out, blend it again, and gently fold it into the stiff whipped whites of four eggs. Cover and return it to the freezer until it is frozen and ready to eat. Serve it in champagne glasses as a cold relief, or use it as a dessert.

Champagne and Carrot Sauce for Venison, Rabbit, Veal, or Game Bird

Melt a stick of butter in a saucepan. Slice thin about a half dozen shallots into the butter and sizzle them until they begin to brown. (Be careful not to burn the butter.) Stir a few tablespoons of flour into the butter and shallots to make a paste. Then add one cup of sliced red onions, a tablespoon of basil, a teaspoon of marjoram, a couple of bay leaves, a cup of peeled and diced carrots, two tablespoons of beef base, a tablespoon each of A1 and Worcestershire sauces, a split of champagne, and half a cup of cognac. Salt and pepper to taste. Simmer until the carrots are soft and then blend them for a few seconds on the lowest speed of the blender so they retain some texture. For the last fifteen minutes of whatever it is that you're baking, remove it from the oven, drain off the grease, then pour the carrot sauce over the meat and return it to the oven, uncovered. When it's done, remove the meat from the pan and place it on a serving platter. Blend the sauce for a second or two, pour it over the entree, and serve.

Carrots Flamed in Brandy

Melt a stick of butter in a frying pan; when it begins to sizzle, turn the heat down and add about two cups of carrots cut into strips. Sprinkle with salt, pepper, and a tablespoon of thyme, and add about a tablespoon of honey and half a cup of red wine. Cover and simmer until the carrots become soft to

(Carrots Flambee)   the touch of the fork; then uncover and let the juice cook down. When almost no juice is left but a thick sauce, heat half a cup of brandy, pour it over the carrots, ignite, and serve.

Carrot Supreme   Peel and slice two cups of carrots, and cook them with one cup of cream sherry over low heat until soft. Then place the entire mixture in the blender and add the yolks of four eggs, two packages of un-flavored gelatin, a quarter cup of frozen orange juice concentrate, and half a cup of honey. Blend until smooth, return to the heat, add a cup of heavy cream, and simmer, stirring constantly until the mixture becomes thick and custardy. Then blend it again and pour it into ice-cube trays; set in the freezer until the mixture is about half frozen. Whip the four egg whites until stiff in one bowl, and a pint of whipping cream in another bowl. Blend the fro-zen mixture in the blender with a cup of Amaretto, then fold it into the egg whites. Then fold that mix-ture into the whipped cream. Place in parfait glasses, and chill for at least an hour before serving.

And those are some of the things you can do with a carrot. You might use the very same recipes substituting pumpkin, banana squash, Blue Hubbard squash, acorn squash, or any of the winter squashes, turnips, parsnips, or even potatoes, if you add enough honey. What is so astonishing is that each vegetable will make the recipe something entirely different. And even more so is the fact that it is not necessary to follow the recipe at all if you don't want to. Change the wines and liqueurs, the spices, the vegetables; make it whatever you like.

Almost no one likes vegetables during childhood. I can remember my mother opening a can of Irish potatoes, slicing them into margarine, and frying them in an aluminum frying pan—even with plenty of salt and pepper and catsup you could not escape the taste of the can. And of course, almost everyone boiled everything. Boiled green beans, boiled potatoes, boiled Brussels sprouts—all the taste and vitamins were poured down the drain.

Like every other kind of food, vegetables can be done in a thousand different and exciting ways; you merely take what you have on hand and work it around. The following are some of the things I "worked around" in the Blue Strawbery kitchen in the past few years.

The simplest way to prepare acorn squash (also called Des Moines squash) is to cut it in half, clean out the seeds, sprinkle the inside with salt and pepper, add a lump of butter, and bake uncovered in a 400° oven for thirty to forty-five minutes. Variations are simple. Sprinkle on some nutmeg or cinnamon ...a little saffron or curry...basil, sage...absolutely any herb you want to try will probably work on the squash. Add a dash of honey, brown sugar, or white sugar, or jelly, jam, molasses, or maple syrup. Experiment with acorn squash baked in plum jam, brandy, and curry.

Baked Acorn Squash

When I make acorn squash in the restaurant I cut them into their natural sections, lay them in a baking pan with the meat side up, pour a sauce over them, cover, and bake. I uncover the squash fifteen or twenty minutes before I serve it and ladle the juices over it to form a glaze.

Put about half a stick of melted butter into the blender, add salt and pepper, about two-thirds of a cup of white wine, and a cup of brown sugar. Blend until smooth, and pour it over the squash sections in a baking pan. Bake covered in a 400° oven for

Brown Sugar Sauce for Acorn Squash

(Brown Sugar Sauce) about half an hour. Uncover, ladle the juices over the squash, and bake uncovered for another fifteen or twenty minutes.

The thing to concern yourself with is how long to bake the squash, covered and uncovered, and what the sauce might be. The sauce can be almost anything you desire. Simply begin with a little melted butter or margarine, and add whatever you have around to make enough sauce to cover the squash. By blending in a little frozen orange juice concentrate, some apricot brandy, and a couple of fresh plums you produce a sauce so elegant that people will talk about it for a long time.

Any sweet glaze you might want to make for squash, carrots, parsnips, or any such vegetable, always begins with the butter. After that it is entirely up to you. You can prove this to yourself; the next time you are fixing winter vegetables, try a new sauce. You can either do this in a blender or not; if you don't use a blender, the consistency of whatever fruit you are using will add still one more dimension to the dish. Lay the vegetables in a baking pan, pour enough butter over them so that they will not stick to the pan (usually half a cup will do it), then add whatever fruit you choose—either a lot or just a little for flavor—and sprinkle with sugar, honey, or any other sweetener. Don't forget salt and pepper; you are preparing a vegetable, not a dessert. Of course sweet potatoes and yams fixed this way are referred to as "candied."

Candied Sweet Potatoes Wash and slice as many sweet potatoes as you'll need and lay them in a baking dish. (It's not necessary to peel them; in fact, if you eat the peels you'll not only be getting more potato for your money, but you'll also be getting a lot of nutrients that would otherwise have been lost. I try not to peel anything if I can help it—bananas I peel.) Then all you have to do is to make about a third of a blenderful of sauce

—a mixture of melted butter, chocolate brandy, and fresh apricots, for example—pour it on, and bake. The combinations can be of any fruit, any liqueur or juice, any spice or herb, any jam or jelly. Sweet potatoes in limes and honey and curry...parsnips in oranges and curry and apricot brandy... turnips and apples in white wine, apple jelly, and brandy.

(Candied Sweet Potatoes)

It's also nice with all these vegetables, after they've baked, to whip them until smooth, as you would mashed potatoes, then add two eggs and bake them another fifteen minutes. Wonderful! No matter what you are adding to your recipe it never takes but a few seconds; so any dish that may sound elaborate might easily take only thirty seconds to put together. I do that all the time: with two people to help me in the kitchen I can prepare food for eighty people in two hours. And at home I can do a dinner for six in less than fifteen minutes. I just try to use the most logical, simple, and easy approach; that's what I'm trying to show you. All you do is put stuff into a blender, whip it up, and it's a sauce. Period. Then all you have to do is pour it on something. Takes all the work out of it—all you have to do is fill the blender, and the more wonderful the things you fill it with, the more incredible the taste of the outcome. And, because you're using fresh foods, it's also good for you.

But we are speaking of vegetables; so I will continue by showing you a few different ways to serve acorn squash.

Angel Squash

Split acorn squash in halves the long way, clean out the seeds, and sprinkle generously with salt, pepper, mace, and lemon juice. Put a lump of butter on top, and bake in a 400° oven until the squash feels soft to the touch of a fork. Remove the squash and carefully scoop out the insides, leaving the shell intact. Mash the squash meat and smooth it in the blender

(Angel Squash)

with an egg yolk and a tablespoon of flour for each squash half, and several shots of apricot brandy. Then whip up the egg whites you have left and carefully fold in the squash mixture. Fill each squash shell with the whipped mixture, return them to the oven, and continue to bake uncovered at 400° for fifteen to twenty minutes. Serve. This could easily become a dessert: just add a tablespoon of any sweetener for each half, and place a scoop of vanilla ice cream in the center of each one just before you serve it.

Acorn Squash Vegetarian

Here is a superb vegetarian entree, complete luncheon, late snack, or whatever. It's also good for people who want to lose weight. Scoop out the insides of the halves of an acorn squash. Then fill them with a mixture of chopped eggplant, zucchini, tomatoes, and peppers. Salt and pepper each one, and sprinkle generously with basil and marjoram. Then place a lump of butter in the center of each squash, and pour enough red, white, or rose wine across the top to drench the stuffing. (The stuffing may either be even with the squash or rise over the top.) Over this place a thin slice of mozzarella, Swiss, or Muenster cheese, and cook it in a 400° oven for thirty to forty-five minutes. The cheese should be brown and crusty on the top. You eat the entire thing and throw the shell away—it's biodegradable! A lovely dish.

You don't have to stay with the four suggested vegetables for a stuffing, of course. You could do all mushrooms, all tomatoes, or a mixture of whatever vegetables you'd like. And if you want, you can always add meat. Stuff the squash with sliced chicken and mushrooms and cover with cheese, put together a little salad, and you've done a lovely luncheon for six people in about fifteen minutes.

There are other ways to cook acorn squash if you don't want it stuffed, glazed, or served with ice cream as a dessert. Try putting some melted butter into the blender with a little white wine and some onions or green vegetables; make it into a sauce, pour it over the squash, cover it, and bake as you would the other dishes. Acorn squash can be anything from soup to dessert, and the exact same thing holds true for all winter squashes, pumpkin, parsnips, carrots, turnips and rutabagas, sweet potatoes and yams. The cost of squash is minimal: you can buy a twenty-pound Blue Hubbard squash for about a nickel a pound. Consider all the dishes you could make, all the people you could feed, for that dollar's worth of squash. (Usually at about this time, some very interested-looking homemaker smiles rather pathetically and says something like, "That's fine for you, but I can't get my family to eat anything but meat and potatoes and frozen dinners." Well, you have only yourself to blame if you allow that to happen. Forgive me; I'm probably the only person in the world that can become messianic in appreciation of Blue Hubbard squash.)

Any Vegetable Cream Sauce

Here's a simple and inexpensive cream sauce to cook all of your vegetables in. Melt half a stick of butter and put it in the blender with about three tablespoons of flour, half a cup of white wine, three cups of milk, and salt and white pepper to taste. You might add some lemon juice to this, or any herb or spice—tarragon, chervil, parsley, bay leaves, allspice. Wash the vegetables to be cooked, cut and trim them if need be, put them into a good-sized saucepan, pour the cream sauce over them, cover, and slowly bring to a simmering boil. Stir it rather often so that the sauce doesn't separate. This is a wonderful sauce for tiny pearl onions.

In the next few pages I will show you some simple ways to make ordinary vegetables—the ones in season, the inexpensive vegetables—taste so novel and exciting that you'll be tempted to eat fresh vegetables all of the time.

Oven Vegetables

The Italians make a dish similar to this called *Vegetale al Forno*; loosely translated, this means "oven vegetables." I try to bake as many vegetables as I can and the only ones that I usually do on top of the stove are green vegetables or those that I happen to be deep frying. For this dish you need a nice-sized baking dish—preferably one you might also serve in. Place on the bottom a layer of thin-sliced eggplant, on top of that a layer of thin-sliced zucchini, then a layer of sliced tomatoes, then sliced peppers. Then take a cup of red wine, mix it with half a cup of melted butter or margarine, about four tablespoons of tamari or soy sauce, some pepper, garlic, oregano, and basil. Pour it over the vegetables, lay slices of Swiss or mozzarella cheese across the top, and bake it uncovered in a 400° oven for forty-five minutes to an hour, depending on the size of the dish. The cheese should be crusty on top. Makes a terrific one-dish meal, or a hot salad (a hot salad!?), a side dish with meat, or just a nice late, light supper with some rose wine.

Curried Cucumbers

Melt half a stick of butter and mix it in the blender with one tablespoon of flour for thickening, a tablespoon of moist chicken base, white pepper to taste, one tablespoon of curry powder, and about three-quarters of a cup of dry white wine. Then peel and slice enough cucumbers for the number of people you wish to serve (figure at least half a cuke per person) and lay them seed side up in a baking dish.

Pour the sauce over, cover, and bake at 400° for about twenty minutes. Then uncover and bake another five to ten minutes.

(Curried Cucumbers)

One good-sized head of cauliflower should easily feed six people as a side dish. It can be simmered on top of the stove, with a cheese sauce poured over the top as you serve it, or it can be baked with the sauce. Here are three sauces to try with basic baked cauliflower.

Break the cauliflower into its natural sections, then wash and lay them in a baking dish. Pour the sauce over, cover, and bake at 400° for half an hour to forty-five minutes, or until it begins to be soft.

Three Sauces for Baked Cauliflower

Chive and White Wine Sauce: Melt half a stick of butter and put it in the blender with a tablespoon of flour for thickening, three-quarters of a cup of white wine, about a tablespoon of moist chicken base, and salt and white pepper to taste. Stir in chopped chives. This should easily be enough sauce for a head of cauliflower.

Caraway and Cheese Sauce: Melt half a stick of butter and put it in the blender with a tablespoon of flour, half a cup of dry white wine, half a cup of milk, about a tablespoon of caraway seeds, and one cup of any kind of grated cheese. Blend well and pour over the cauliflower.

Tomato, Lemon, and Grand Marnier Sauce: In the blender place a whole tomato, a shot of Grand Marnier, half a stick of melted butter, salt and white pepper, some parsley, and the juice of one lemon. Blend for a few seconds on the slowest speed so that the tomato retains a little texture. Pour over the cauliflower.

Spinach, beet greens, collard greens, mustard greens, cauliflower greens, and any other kind of greens first should be trimmed and washed. Then put them into a pot, add about a cup of white or red wine or tomato juice, salt, pepper, and maybe a little garlic, and simmer them until they become limp. It takes almost no time at all. Remember that greens always shrink a lot, so you'll need about three times the amount you would use if it were any other vegetable. You might chop hard-boiled eggs across the greens just before you serve them, or squeeze a lemon, lime, or orange over them.

Potatoes Stuffed with Greens

Take any of the raw greens mentioned above and chop them into small pieces, then cook them and drain them. Bake several large Idaho potatoes, and when they are done cut them into halves the long way and scoop out the potato meat. Into this, mash the cooked greens; then stuff the mixture back into the potato skins. Bake uncovered at 400° for fifteen to twenty minutes.

Or, if you are making a cream soup for your first course, you can use the scooped-out potato meat for the thickening, and then add a couple of egg yolks to the greens. Mix in a little flour or breadcrumbs for binding. Then whip the egg whites into peaks, and carefully fold in the greens and egg mixture. Pile it back into the potato skins and cook it at 400° for fifteen or twenty minutes.

ZUCCHINI, EGGPLANT, AND SUMMER SQUASH

Zucchini, yellow summer squash, and eggplant are all varieties of summer squashes. There's no need to peel them; simply slice on an angle in thin slices, dip in whipped eggs and then in breadcrumbs, and place gently in about half an inch of hot grease in a frying pan. Brown them on both sides, salt and pepper them, and serve. This is my favorite way to cook summer squashes, but there are many others.

You can slice the squash, lay it in a baking pan, and pour a sauce over it. Then bake it uncovered in a 400° oven, basting occasionally, for half an hour to forty-five minutes. Sauces for squash begin with a little melted butter or margarine and progress from there; adding a cup of yogurt, some dill, salt, and white pepper to melted butter is terrific on any of the aforementioned squashes. So is yogurt and tomatoes and dill, or basil, or curry. And, naturally, just about any of the sauces will work on any other vegetable.

Another delicious way to make zucchini, eggplant, and summer squash is to stuff them.

Baked Stuffed Zucchini, Eggplant, or Summer Squash

Split the vegetable in half the long way, and scoop out the insides into sizzling butter in a frying pan, leaving anywhere from half an inch to an inch of meat still in the shell. Fry the squash meat until it becomes soft, adding salt and pepper and any herbs you might like. Then scoop it into a mixing bowl together with the juices and butter from frying, and add an egg or two. To this mixture you can add whatever you please: cooked shrimp, langostinos, or crabmeat; or other vegetables such as tomatoes, onions, mushrooms, or celery. Chop as much or as little as you like into the cooked meat of the squash, and add enough breadcrumbs to hold it all together. Taste it now and again to be certain it has enough seasoning for your liking; you might also want to add a few splashes of wine or sherry. Then fill the cavities of the squash or eggplant, sprinkle the top with lemon juice and Parmesan cheese, and bake in a 400° oven for thirty to forty-five minutes, depending on the size of the vegetable.

Some zucchini grow to be as large as twelve pounds. To have one of those split in half, stuffed with a lot of incredible things, and served with a sauce over it to a large group would save you time, trouble, and expense.

Baked Zucchini Stuffed with Shrimp

Stuff a zucchini with shrimp according to the directions above. As it bakes, melt a stick of butter and put it in the blender with one cup of white wine, two tomatoes, a tablespoon of moist chicken base, some white pepper, basil, and lemon juice. Blend it on the slowest speed so that the sauce has a texture of tomatoes in it, and simmer it for twenty to thirty minutes before you pour it over the stuffed vegetable.

You could also stuff the smaller variety of zucchini, squash, or eggplant, and make individual servings. Or, instead of tomatoes in the sauce described above, use fresh broccoli, or asparagus, or mushrooms, or simply onions. You need to have confidence that everything will work. Once you assure yourself of that fact the mixtures of sauces and ingredients will come more easily each time you attempt a meal. And even if the cost of some wines or liqueurs makes some things I have described prohibitive, you could substitute any juices you might have around. Tomato juice, vegetable juices, milk, beer, bouillons, and consomme will all work. But anything will work only so far as your personal taste will allow it to work. (Aha...a lesson in life.) If something doesn't taste right to you before you cook it, or serve it, or ladle it over something, then work it around—taste what is lacking and don't be afraid to experiment. If a sauce or dish tastes bland, more than likely all it needs is a little more salt or a little more wine, or a little more of any of the ingredients you've happened to put together. Just keep tasting something until it begins to taste good. It will taste even better after it's cooked. That's cooking.

Leaving the peel on the eggplant, slice it and lay it domino-style in a baking pan. Then mix in a blender one melted stick of butter, two cups of burgundy, half a pound of grated mozzarella cheese, a tablespoon of curry, a tablespoon of moist chicken base, a teaspoon of savory, and salt and white pepper to taste. Pour over the eggplant, and bake covered in a 425° oven for forty-five minutes.

**Eggplant
in a Curry
Cheese Sauce**

If you're figuring on six people, and you're serving a roast loin of pork, baked apples will be the perfect accompaniment to the dinner.

Core six apples, lay them in a baking pan, sprinkle them with brown sugar and allspice, and bake them in a 400° oven for about fifteen minutes. While they are baking, prepare the glaze. In a blender mix two cups of fresh cranberries, or a can of whole cranberry sauce, a cup of brandy, a small can of frozen orange juice concentrate, and a little cinnamon and cloves. Blend it until smooth, pour it over the apples, and let them bake another fifteen to twenty minutes.

**Baked Apple
in a Cranberry
and Brandy Glaze**

Baked Corn on the Cob. Grow your own corn, pick it, husk it as you're running to the kitchen, plunge it into boiling water for three to four minutes, and immediately serve with butter. Then you are eating corn. But not everyone has the pleasure of his or her own garden, and there are other ways to fix corn that is not quite so fresh. Husk the corn and lay the ears in a baking pan with a tight cover. Then make a mixture of melted butter, nutmeg, salt and pepper, and a little white wine, and pour it over the corn. Make sure it's tightly sealed—tin foil will do—then bake at 500° for about fifteen minutes. You could change the nutmeg to anything else that you might prefer, or substitute for the white wine any exotic liqueur that you like—coffee brandy, chocolate brandy, apricot brandy, a little bourbon... Even with no liquor at all, just the salt, pepper, and butter will still produce a lovely dish.

Corn off the cob can be made into many things, not the least being creamed corn. (If you have an electric knife you'll find it invaluable for taking corn off the cob. Simply start at the top of the ear and cut down; about four times around the cob will clean it.)

Creamed Corn Baked with Sherry

Remove the corn from the cob and run half of it through a blender on the slowest speed with a tablespoon or two of honey, salt and white pepper, a splash of cream sherry, and about a quarter cup of heavy cream. Then mix it with the whole kernels of corn and either cook it in a covered saucepan, stirring often, for twenty or thirty minutes, or put it in a baking pan, dot it with butter, and bake it uncovered in a 400° oven for about half an hour. You might add some allspice, or nutmeg, cinnamon, sweet basil, parsley, or cardamom...curry would be really exceptional on creamed corn. Just keep trying out different herbs, other kinds of sweeteners, maybe a brandy. If it's too thin you could add a little flour to the corn you are blending.

Onions Flambee

This is best if you can use the little white pearl onions that are about an inch to an inch and a half in diameter; if you can't find them, pick out the smallest yellow onions you can find. They will work almost as well. Peel the onions first; then melt about a stick of butter until sizzling in a frying pan and put in the onions. Sprinkle them with salt, pepper, sugar, and thyme, and let them cook on a rather low flame until they begin to brown on all sides. When you feel the onions are cooked, turn the heat up as high as it will go, splash in a little brandy, and ignite it. Serve the onions flaming in the frying pan if it's at all possible.

(Onions Flambee)

This whole idea of setting food aflame goes much further than the predictable tournedos and crepes and desserts. Fruits and vegetables flambee can suddenly become an entirely different prospect. I often flame parsnips and carrots, onions, sweet potatoes, or celery . . . With almost anything that you think would be nice set afire, simply splash a little heated brandy or cognac over the top and light it.

POTATOES

The poor, misused, misunderstood, taken-for-granted potato. I am astonished to think of how often it is simply boiled, baked, fried, or mashed with no imagination whatsoever. To boil a potato and then mash it is insultingly mundane; but who doesn't like mashed potatoes? The next time you make them, bake the potatoes in their skins until soft, then scoop the meat out of the skins, add milk and butter and salt and pepper, and mash them that way. Much more taste and much better for you. And mashed potatoes are the ideal food for trying out a spice that you haven't used before. Add it to the potato when you are mashing it. Try caraway seeds, or basil, or saffron. And if you have no gravy use a little butter and sour cream and chives — these things don't always have to fall upon the center of a baked potato. Or, after you've mashed the potatoes, add a couple of egg yolks to them, whip until smooth, then whip the egg whites until stiff and blend the potatoes into that and bake them for another fifteen minutes. Sprinkle a little white wine across them, or lemon-flavored bread-crumbs, or Parmesan cheese, or grated Swiss or Muenster cheese, or a combination of grated cheese and chopped onions and chives or scallions.

Potatoes in a Brown Wine Sauce

Wash and slice as many potatoes as you'll need into a baking pan. Then melt half a stick of butter and put it in a blender with an onion, about a cup of burgundy, enough beef bouillon to give it base and flavor, some black pepper, and about two table-spoons of flour. Blend that until smooth, pour it over the sliced potatoes, cover tightly, and bake at 400° for about forty-five minutes. It's good to take the cover off for the last fifteen or twenty minutes and mix the potatoes around in the sauce so that they'll brown on the edges.

Of course, the sauce may be changed in many different ways. You could add cheese to it, or tomatoes, sour cream, heavy cream, or beer. Or you can substitute apples and turnips for the potatoes for an entirely new dish. What makes this dish so terrific is that you can prepare it in about three minutes. I suppose another thing that keeps cooking so interesting and enjoyable for me is that nothing takes hours and hours of preparation. You simply don't have to do that at all if you continue to use your imagination. I can imagine how awful it would be to have five or six people for dinner and to be continually running in and out of the kitchen, checking on this, pushing that around, plus trying to look attractive in something doubleknit . . . the entire prospect looms as an unhappy occasion. Once you begin to plan what you'd like to serve for a dinner, it's easy enough to arrange an entire menu that all happens at the same time. All the host or hostess should have to do is walk in and serve it, remove dishes, and bring on whatever is next. But you should also be able to sit down and eat each course with your guests without feeling rushed or crammed. The best way to begin that is to get everything ready and know exactly what time to put things in the oven. Not hard to do. But then this is supposed to be about different kinds of potatoes.

Everyone knows that if you bake potatoes in milk and onions

and cheese you'll have a variety of creamed potatoes (or "potatoes au gratin," or Lyonnaise potatoes), but after doing potatoes that way once I felt compelled to see what else I could get out of the idea. Recently I tried it this way:

Peel spuds and place them in a baking pan. Then mix in a blender enough melted butter, white wine, chicken stock, saffron, and white pepper to pour over the potatoes and leave about an inch of sauce on the bottom of the pan. Cover the potatoes and bake them at 400° for about forty-five minutes. Then take them out of the oven and drain all the sauce into the blender. Add two or three of the small cooked potatoes, one egg, and a little heavy cream; whip it until smooth; pour it back over the potatoes; and put it all back into the oven, uncovered, for another fifteen to twenty minutes.

**Potatoes
in a Potato Sauce**

I can't tell you how lovely the outcome was. Because of the egg and the cream, the sauce puffed up and turned brown on the tops of the potatoes, leaving a creamy hollow place before the potato itself began. And the sauce was perfect for the potato.

You could do potato that same way, only changing the ingredients in the sauce almost indefinitely. Some of the combinations would stagger the mind. Smoked Edam cheese, sherry, and sour cream...vodka, chives, and yogurt...tomatoes, caraway, and burgundy...each of these combinations mixed with a little butter and salt and pepper will turn the most ordinary potato into a new sensual pleasure. And consider that anything you can do with a potato you can also do with a parsnip, rutabaga, sweet potato, or yam. Isn't that a wonderful fact? You've just learned how to do fifteen sauces for six different vegetables.

Potato Chips: I often make homemade potato chips at Blue Strawbery; to serve a hot potato chip, fresh out of the pot, is truly a lovely gesture in these days of instant foods — and very simple to do. You ought to try it for the fun of it; it is fun, and the results will make everyone joyful. Begin with a few large white or red potatoes; don't feel as though you have to peel them — I never peel potatoes that I use for chips or French fries. Poke a fork into one end of the potato to make it easier to cut, and with a sharp knife slice the potato as thin as you possibly can. You'll be surprised to see how thin you can cut them after the first two or three. And if they are a little thick it's all right, they'll taste good too. Dry them, and fry them in a deep-fat fryer, or just a simple pot with a lot of hot oil or lard. (Lard does a pretty nice thing to potato chips and particularly to French fries. Lard makes them taste like they did in the fifties.)

French Fries: When I was a little boy living in Oak Park, Illinois my family used to take me on rare occasions to the local Chinese restaurant. All the booths were high, almost to the ceiling, with little lamp shades on the sconces; and all the waiters wore long white aprons. It was the kind of restaurant that served not only Chinese but also American cooking — not like the Chinese-American cooking you get these days, but wonderful food. One of their best dishes was French fries. They simply took a good-sized potato, cut it into quarters, and deep fried it. So when I make them now, I also cut them into quarters, and I never bother to peel them. Not peeling your French fries really makes them delicious and even sneaks a little good health in on you. The choice of oil or fat that you use to fry them has a lot to do with it. French fries done in pure olive oil, to my taste, are certainly extraordinary; but don't look for lightness and an ungreasy taste. Soy oil is good and light; I find corn oil boring; but we all have a favorite oil because we all have different taste, so by all means use whatever it is that you feel most comfortable with.

I am crazy for pizza; but the kind of pizza I used to eat as a kid growing up in Chicago seems to have disappeared off the face of the earth. Pizza used to be such a complete and wonderful thing. But present-day pizza makers have managed to do to the pizza what MacDonald's has done to the hamburger. It's really sad that there are generations of people who will never know what a hamburger really was, or what real pizza is. Well, that's what they call progress. Isn't it strange.

Anyway, it occurred to me that a tomatoless pizza would be something else again. I call it Portsmouth Pie, and it is very simple. This should easily fill up six people for a lunch or late dinner.

Portsmouth Pie

Melt half a stick of butter and put it in the blender with a couple of tablespoons of olive oil, two packages of dry yeast, two eggs, a little salt and sugar, and about a cup of warm milk. Whip it up; then put two to three cups of flour in a bowl and slowly spill in enough of the milk and egg mixture to create a dough. Knead it a little to make sure it's all nicely put together, and then put it in a warm place covered with a towel for about half an hour, just long enough to let it rise. It will rise fast because of the yeast and the eggs. While the dough is rising, slice up a pound of mushrooms and brown them in butter with some salt and pepper and garlic and parsley. You might splash them with some wine or sherry if you like. When they are cooked put them aside. Any juices left in the pan can be used for a sauce. Then cut up a can of hearts of palm into thin slices. (I realize you might not happen to have a can of hearts of palm lying around next to the peanut butter; you can also use a big yellow onion cut into thin, thin slices.) Then put that to the side.

The next thing you have to do is make the sauce. Instead of making a tomato sauce, put four eggs into the blender with the leftover juice from the

(Portsmouth Pie) fried mushrooms, a dash of moist chicken base for a salt, a little flour, white pepper, a little nutmeg, about half a cup of Gruyere cheese, and some white wine just to make it pliable. The sauce should be a little on the thick side. Blend it and put it on a medium flame for about ten minutes, stirring constantly so that the eggs don't stick or burn. Then run it through the blender one more time to smooth it out.

Then take your dough, punch it down, and roll it as thin as you can without tearing it. You'll want to lay it on a good-sized cookie sheet, working it around with your hands until the cookie sheet is covered, and pinching the dough up along the sides. Sprinkle it with a little pepper and basil, lay the mushrooms down, and then the hearts of palm. Then I sprinkle the top with langostinos—you could also use shrimp. Pour the cheese and egg mixture across the top as evenly as you can and sprinkle on enough grated Swiss cheese almost to make a layer. Put it into a 400° oven for about thirty minutes or until it is bubbling and hot.

Portsmouth Pie truly is a lovely dish and astoundingly easy. I suppose it's similar to a quiche, or a cross between a quiche and a pizza. You can use anything on the top that you have on hand: you could do it with all onions, or sliced tomatoes, and it's a perfect vegetarian entree, lunch, snack, appetizer, or late supper. Wouldn't it be lovely about midnight, with a cold bottle of very dry white wine and a salad?

There are a few things to know about taking the ordinary vegetable from being mundane to being something special. For instance, throw in a handful of coconut or raisins when making lima beans...or use orange juice on asparagus or spinach or Brussels sprouts instead of the ordinary lemon juice...or cut tomatoes in half and sprinkle them with pumpkin pie spices and sugar and a little white wine. You can add a handful or two of almonds to just about anything and it will become an "almond-ine." And when I make rice I almost always cut a citrus fruit in half and place it in the water before I start to boil it, leaving it there for the entire time the rice is cooking. Orange, lime, lemon, or grapefruit not only adds a lovely flavor to the rice but the citrus oils keep it a little fluffier and not sticky. Any nuts— almonds, cashews, walnuts, even peanut butter—added to whipped cooked winter squash will also add an uncommon dimension.

Is it really that elementary to arrive at parsnips roasted in oranges and curry and flamed in apricot brandy? The ingredients provide all the clues; it is a simple progression to the end result. Peel the parsnips and lay them in a baking pan, sprinkle them with orange juice and butter and curry, cover them, and bake them until they are soft; then place them in a frying pan, pour hot apricot brandy over them, and ignite. A natural and simple progression. Merely take what you have and put it on something—plums or peaches or apricots or oranges or blueberries or apples, on squash or carrots or parsnips or sweet potatoes... On green vegetables, put butter and whatever else strikes your fancy—nuts, fruit juices, coconut, or a cream sauce. Chop and cook them and stuff them into tomatoes or potatoes or squash. Slice them and bread them and fry them, sprinkle a juice on them. Vegetables can be anything that you have the imagination and courage to make them, and the more times you rely on your imagination, the more fearless and brilliant you'll become in the kitchen.

Batters and Doughs

The secret of a great pancake is really no great secret. You need flour and an egg or two and a little shortening and some liquid — milk, buttermilk, sour cream, heavy cream, or yogurt — and a little baking powder. If you make the batter thick the pancakes will be large and thick and probably heavy, even with the baking powder. If you make the batter too thin, just fry them thin and you'll have crepes. In that case fill them with jelly, roll them up, and sprinkle lemon juice and powdered sugar across the top. Or stuff them with fresh fruit, melt down a pint of ice cream, and serve them with hot melted ice cream across the top. If you're very sneaky you can really knock people out with pancakes first thing in the morning. No matter what you do to the batter, as long as you add a little baking powder, it will turn into some kind of pancake. And the addition of a handful of chopped fresh fruit or vegetables will also make the "cake" an entirely different proposition.

In a bowl combine two duck eggs, one cup of yogurt, two tablespoons of molasses, a dash of salt, one and a half cups of all-purpose flour, one table-spoon of grated orange rind, two teaspoons of baking powder, and one tablespoon of honey. Mix well and drop in spoonfuls onto a lightly greased hot griddle. The pancakes should be about four inches in diameter. Brown on both sides, place on a plate, and top with whipped cream sweetened with maple syrup and mixed with hulled and sliced strawber-ries.

South Berwick Strawberry Pancakes

The following recipe for Polish Doughnuts should yield approximately three dozen doughnuts at a cost of about a dollar and thirty-five cents.

Preheat grease to 450° in a deep-frying pan. In a mixing bowl, combine two eggs, two tablespoons of orange, lemon, or lime rind (or a combination of all three), one pint of whipping cream, three to four teaspoons of baking powder, three to four cups of all-purpose flour, and a dash each of salt and sugar. Mix until the dough becomes sticky, then knead in enough flour to make it dry. Roll out the dough to a thickness of about a quarter inch, and cut it into long strips. Cut each strip into a piece about three inches long. Then make a small cut through its center, twist the end through the center, and drop it into the hot grease.

Fry the doughnuts to a golden brown on both sides, then remove and let drain for a few minutes. Roll them in confectioner's sugar, or cinnamon and sugar, or vanilla and sugar. When one batch of

Polish Doughnuts

doughnuts is done and removed, be careful to give the grease a few moments to get hot again for the next batch. Otherwise the doughnuts might get a little greasy.

It's very easy to vary this recipe—try cutting the dough in circles and putting a spoonful of your favorite jam in each. Then fold half the circle over, pinch down the edges, and fry until golden brown. For use as an appetizer, you can fill the dough with shrimp, crabmeat, tuna, or salmon, and serve with a light sauce.

Four-Minute Dumplings

In a mixing bowl stir together two eggs, three-quarters of a cup of milk, two cups of flour, six teaspoons of baking powder, and a little salt and pepper. Bring about an inch of water to a boil in the bottom of a frying pan and add a spoonful of butter. When the water is boiling moderately drop in spoonfuls of the dumpling batter, leaving room between each one for them to rise, and then cover them for two minutes. Turn them over and cover them again for two minutes. They are then ready to serve with a stew, cream sauce, soup, or any leftover that you want to stretch.

Like the rest of the basics that I've tried to share with you, the dumpling may be modified and changed into several things. For instance, instead of adding two cups of flour add only a cup and a half and then a ripe avocado. The result, of course, is "avocado dumplings." The same idea will work using a cup of cooked shrimp, langostinos, lobster, crabmeat, cooked mushrooms, broccoli, or spinach. The alternatives are legion.

Any noodles will work with the sauce given on the next page for "Noodles High," though I tend to favor spinach noodles over the ordinary. But wide or thin noodles, shells, ribbons, or fettu-ccini will work as well. Noodles should be put in a large pot filled with boiling water, a little salt, and some oil. The oil will keep the noodles from sticking and the largeness of the pot gives them room to move around while they are boiling. The same principle works for any pasta you are cooking. Never cook noodles longer than about twelve minutes; depending on the size of the noodle, the time might be less. Taste them: they should never be soft and mushy, always firm or *al dente* (a little "to the tooth"). The sauce should be made before the noodles are cooked so that when they are done you can drain them, mix in the sauce, and serve immediately. You really can't let noodles sit around in a sauce for very long or they'll become mushy and boring. The following will make enough sauce to serve six people.

Noodles High

Melt a stick of butter in a saucepan and add a couple of tablespoons of flour. Then add garlic powder—the amount is up to you. (I suggest a tablespoonful; that may seem like a lot of garlic but it's the way I like it. That might just explain why I'm still sitting at a little table for one in the corner when I go out to eat.) At any rate, add the same amount of basil, oregano, and marjoram, white pepper to taste, and a little salt. Then add a splash of white wine, a splash of white vermouth, the juice of a lemon, and a pint of sour cream. Stir it around and let it cook slowly. As with anything containing cream, if you boil it too fast it will tend to separate. If it does just put it into a blender or use a whisk until it comes together again. If it is too thick add a little more white wine; if it's too thin add some more sour cream, or a little flour, or an egg to thicken it. When the sauce is bubbling add about a cup of grated Parmesan cheese. Stir well and pour over cooked noodles.

BISCUITS

My grandmother always made baking-powder biscuits. They were so simple I learned to do them myself at the age of six: a cup of milk, two cups of flour, and a few teaspoons of baking powder. Mix these three ingredients in a bowl, drop them by spoonfuls onto a buttered pan, and bake them in a 400° oven for twelve to fifteen minutes. Grandma also put a spoonful of sugar and a sprinkle or two of salt into the mixture. They were—and still are —simple, fast, and terrific. Some years later I learned this Shaker recipe for whipped-cream biscuits:

Shaker Whipped-Cream Biscuits

Whip a cup of heavy cream until stiff, and gently fold in two cups of flour, three teaspoons of baking powder, and a dash of sugar. Knead the dough on a floured board about eight times, roll it to about a quarter-inch thickness, and cut out biscuits. (You can use an ordinary water glass with its edge dipped in flour as your cutter.) Bake them at 400° for about twelve minutes. You needn't even grease the pan because the whipped cream has all the shortening in it.

This wonderful dough can become many things. If you're making biscuits, try dropping in a spoonful of honey and a dash of salt and maybe a little grated orange or lemon rind, or some sesame or caraway seeds—anywhere from a teaspoonful to a tablespoonful. Or you might add a little more sweetening (white sugar is good) to the dough mix, roll it thin, and make it into a pie crust. Then bake it in the pie tin for ten to twelve minutes, let it cool, and fill it with any icebox pie recipe that you like. Or, roll the dough thin, cut larger-size rounds from it, and fill them with jelly, jam, or cooked meat, vegetables, or fish. Then fold the other half of the round over it and press the ends together with a floured fork. They become like *empanada*, Spanish meat-filled pastries. Or, roll the dough thin and long, smooth melted butter across it, sprinkle it with cinnamon and sugar, then roll it up like a jelly cake, cut off one-inch-thick pieces, lay them on their sides in an ungreased baking pan, flatten them out with the palm of your hand, and bake them for twelve to fifteen minutes. They are wonderful in the morning.

The variations of the "one-two-three" method of making biscuits—one cup of liquid, two cups of flour, and three teaspoons of baking powder—are easy to master. Instead of whipping cream just use milk, yogurt, clabbered milk (that's milk that has become a little sour), or sour cream. To any of those liquids you could also add a splash or two of wine or sherry—a cream sherry and a little honey used with sour cream is just fantastic—and you could try other flours. Mix in a little whole-wheat pastry flour with the white flour, or a rye flour with the white. Mixing rye with white flour, a little honey, sour cream, and some grated orange rind will throw you a biscuit you'll not forget for a long time. In the event that you are not using a heavy cream—whipped or not—it's good to add a tablespoon or so of shortening to the recipe and to lightly butter the baking pan. A tablespoon of duck fat is really nice (if you're cooking a duck and happen to have some around) but, by and large, butter or margarine will do just fine. As long as you remember the basic one-two-three plan you'll always get a perfect dough. It never fails.

Desserts

Several years ago I worked as a waiter in a restaurant that served French pastries. It took me about two weeks to get over pastries for the rest of my life. At Blue Strawbery we serve strawberries with sour cream and brown sugar in lieu of pastries for dessert. Naturally, you leave them whole (of course we only use fresh strawberries) and you dip them in sour cream, then the brown sugar, and as quickly as possible put them into your mouth. The dessert works equally well with green grapes, quartered peaches, plums, fresh pineapple—whatever fresh fruit you happen to have. For the kind of dinner I cook it seems to be the most complementary and sensible dessert.

There are some times of year that I simply cannot procure fresh strawberries, and don't feel like pineapples; or I just get the urge to be a little more creative than the sour cream and brown sugar approach. Having never studied cooking, I had to invent my own mousse, souffle, ice cream, sherbet, pudding—all those things that people call desserts. The concept of a mousse, or what I refer to as a mousse, came very easily. Whether or not it is an authentic mousse is of little consequence to me, or, I hope, to you. If it is important you'd better get yourself a cookbook that teaches that sort of thing. If, however, you prefer to be more creative, and have a little courage, then you might try a few of the following.

Fruit Mousse

You'll need eggs, some unflavored gelatin, heavy cream for whipping, fruit for flavoring, and a sweetening. I find a blender invaluable when making this dessert. It will save you all kinds of time and make it so much easier you'll begin to make mousse all the time. Separate six eggs and blend the yolks with a cup of cream sherry and three packages of unflavored gelatin. Cook that over moderate-to-low heat, stirring constantly so that the eggs don't stick; bring it to a boil and let it thicken like a custard. Then pour it back into the blender and add a cup of white wine and two cups of any fruit. (The fruit should be pitted but don't peel it.) Blend until smooth, then set it aside to cool. Whip up the egg whites and slowly mix in the egg-and-fruit mixture. Then whip a pint of heavy cream and add half a cup of honey to it. Combine the two mixtures and set in the refrigerator to cool. Put it either into a large bowl or into individual serving dishes or parfait or wine glasses. Let it sit for an hour or so and serve.

Citrus Mousse

Separate six eggs and place the yolks in a blender. Add three packages of unflavored gelatin, a cup of heavy cream, and a quarter cup of apricot brandy. Blend until smooth and then place over moderate heat and bring to a boil; turn the heat down, stirring constantly, and let the mixture simmer until it becomes thick and syrupy. Put it back in the blender, add the juice of one lemon, the juice of two

(Citrus Mousse)

limes, a small can of frozen orange juice concentrate, and half a cup of honey. Blend until smooth, pour into a bowl, and set it in the freezer until it is cold and beginning to frost on the sides. Remove it, whip up the egg whites, put the mousse through the blender again, and then fold it slowly into the whipped egg whites. Place in glasses and set in the refrigerator to cool.

Chocolate Mousse

Separate six eggs, put the yolks in the blender, and add three packages of unflavored gelatin, half a cup of chocolate brandy, three tablespoons of powdered baking chocolate, and half a cup of honey; blend until smooth. Set on moderate heat and, stirring constantly, bring the mixture to a slow boil; it should become thick and syrupy. Remove it from the heat and puree it in the blender again. Then set it in the refrigerator to cool. Whip up the egg whites and fold the cooled mixture into them. Then put a quarter of a cup of heavy cream into the blender, add a shot of chocolate brandy and two crumbled-up milk-chocolate bars, with or without nuts, and blend. The mixture does not have to be smooth; little bits of chocolate and nuts will add texture. Combine the two mixtures thoroughly. Then whip the rest of the cream into stiff peaks, and fold the chocolate mixture into it. Set in the refrigerator to cool; sprinkle the top with grated chocolate and nuts.

It should be obvious by now that you begin the mousse by blending six egg yolks with a cup of liquid. (You might use a cream sherry, a white wine, Madeira, or heavy cream.) Then you add three packages of unflavored gelatin and half a cup of sweetening—honey, white sugar, brown sugar, jam, or jelly. Boil the mixture until it becomes thick—it should take about ten minutes.

Taste it at this point to see if it might need more sweetening; perhaps you like your desserts sweeter than I do. If so, keep adding sugar a little at a time until it tastes to you like a good, sweet dessert. Pour the mixture back into the blender and add your flavoring—vanilla with white wine or cream sherry, chocolate with chocolate brandy or apricot brandy or Cointreau. Coffee brandy will give you a mocha mousse. Keep tasting the mixture in the blender; add more chocolate or vanilla, or concentrated frozen orange juice with chocolate, or a few teaspoons of instant coffee. Blend it until smooth, let it cool, then whip it into the six egg whites (which you have whipped), then into a pint of whipped cream. At this point, before you put it in the refrigerator to cool, you might add a cup of blueberries, blackberries, or raspberries, or a cup of any chopped fruit. Also, if you like, the mousse can be put in the freezer and covered until frozen. It then becomes an ice cream—certainly not the kind that takes hours to churn, but a very different kind that can be called either ice cream or frozen mousse.

Pumpkin pudding may be served hot, cold, or frozen, with or without a glob of whipped cream on the top. I make it because I can remember that as a kid I loved pumpkin pie but hated the crust. I am not alone in that bias—just ask any kid how he likes pie crust.

Pumpkin Pudding

You'll need two cups of cooked pumpkin meat. Blend it into four eggs, one pint of heavy cream, a cup of cream sherry, a cup of honey, a small can of frozen orange juice concentrate, a cup of chopped walnuts, and a quarter cup of flour. Put it into a baking pan and bake at 375° for forty-five minutes. Scoop it into dishes and serve. Or let it cool and serve it with orange-flavored whipped cream, or lemon-flavored whipped cream. Or serve it frozen.

Menus

U sing the basic concepts from the previous chapters and a little help as to ingredients on certain dishes, you should be able to put together dinners to please even the fussiest gourmet. As I've said, when we first opened the Blue Strawbery I had never had any experience in cooking this kind of food. I simply went in and used my sense of logic, and a lot of imagination. The same should be possible for you.

Most of the dishes in these menus either are included in the text or are variations on those in the text. They are ideas for you to work around according to your taste and what is in your cupboard. If you need guidelines, you should be able to find them by checking the index of this book.

•

Hot Collard Green Cream Soup
Cranshaw Melon Slices
Tenderloin of Beef in a Pumpkin Sauce
Fresh Broccoli
Tomato Halves Baked with Red Wine, Parmesan Cheese, and Dill
Strawberries, Brown Sugar, and Sour Cream

•

White Onion and Saffron Cream Soup
Frogs' Legs in Tomatoes and Grand Marnier
Fresh Spinach Salad with a Lime Dressing
Cornish Hens in Champagne and Sour Cream
French Fried Eggplant
Noodles in a White Wine, Asparagus, and Cheese Sauce
Acorn Squash in Limes and Curry
Citrus Mousse

•

Broccoli and White Wine Cream Soup
Fisherman's Casserole
Honeydew Melon with Lebanon Bologna and Lime Juice
Roast Leg of Veal in a Cucumber Sauce
Fresh Asparagus
Potatoes Roasted in White Wine and Caraway
Tomatoes Baked in Anisette
Mangoes, Sour Cream, and Brown Sugar

•

Baked Oven Vegetable Soup, Topped with Swiss Cheese
Stuffed Mushrooms
Romaine Leaves in a Sour Cream and Roquefort Dressing
Crab Legs in a Golden Cream Sauce
Brussels Sprouts Sauteed in Butter
Baked Potato Stuffed with Spinach
Carrots Roasted in Oranges and Curry and Coffee Brandy
Captain Midnight Mousse (made with Ovaltine)

•

White Onion and Corn Chowder
Stuffed Mushrooms
Cucumbers in an Orange Vinaigrette
Chicken Breast Stuffed with Prosciutto in Red Wine and Tomatoes
Fresh Broccoli
Peeled Potatoes in White Wine, Parsley, Salt, and Pepper
Baked Fruit in Brandy, Orange Juice, and Brown Sugar

•

Asparagus Cream Soup
Quail's Eggs on Lettuce in a Green Vodka Sauce
Summer Snow
Cornish Hens Wrapped in Ham in a Sour Cream and Sherry Sauce
Oven Vegetables
Lime and Saffron Pilaf
Corn on the Cob in Honey, Nutmeg, Salt, and Pepper
Pineapple, Brown Sugar, and Sour Cream

•

Baked Fruit-of-the-Sea Stew
Mushroom Caps Baked in Ricotta and Brandy
Spinach in a Caviar Caesar Dressing
Leg of Lamb in Pumpkin, Honey, and Soy Sauce
Fresh Asparagus
Mashed Potatoes in Sour Cream, Chicken Bouillon, and Chives
Baked Green Tomatoes in Lemon Juice and Grated Cheddar Cheese
Raspberry Souffle

•

Chilled Salmon in Mayonnaise and Capers, Garnished with Quail's Eggs
Chicken and White Wine Broth with Apple Bits
Chopped Hearts of Palm Vinaigrette
Roast Loin of Pork in Sour Cream, Sauerkraut, and Mushrooms
Pearl Onions Flambee
Fresh String Beans
Baked Peaches
Citrus Mousse

•

Cream of Leek Soup
Shrimp Stuffed Mushrooms
Spinach Salad
Pheasant in Chocolate Brandy and Sour Cream
Apples and Turnips in a Brown Wine Sauce
Sliced, Breaded, and Fried Green Tomatoes
Dumplings in a Butter and White Wine Sauce
White Grapes, Sour Cream, and Brown Sugar

•

Wine Broth Supreme with Homemade Ginger Noodles
Crepes Stuffed with Shrimp, Crabmeat, and Salmon
Belgian Endive in an Avocado Mousse
Roast Loin of Pork in Mushrooms, Red Wine, and Sauerkraut
Acorn Squash in an Orange, Nutmeg, and Port Wine Sauce
Sauteed Green Beans
Noodles High
Strawberries, Brown Sugar, and Sour Cream

•

Butternut Squash Cream Soup
Baked Mushrooms in a Wine and Shrimp Sauce
Fresh Melon
Baked Salmon in a Sauce Marguerite
Breaded and Fried Sliced Zucchini
Tomatoes Baked in Parmesan Cheese and Rose Wine
Sliced Potatoes Roasted in Red Wine, Beef Bouillon, and Onions
White Grapes, Sour Cream, and Brown Sugar

•

Carrot and Saffron Cream Soup
Frogs' Legs in White Wine and Basil Sauce
Romaine Leaves in a Mango Dressing
Striped Bass in a Crabmeat and Shrimp Sauce
Sweet Potatoes in Plums, Honey, Orange, and Red Wine
Cauliflower in White Wine and Caraway
Brussels Sprouts
Cranberry Mousse

•

Blue Hubbard Squash Cream Soup
Crab Stuffed Mushrooms
Spinach Salad in a Lime and Sour Cream Dressing
Tenderloin of Beef in Mushrooms and Rose Wine
Potatoes and Cabbage Baked in Red Wine
Acorn Squash in Ginger and Oranges
Sauteed Fresh Asparagus
Strawberry Chocolate Mousse

•

Baked Spinach and Wine Broth Garnished with Chopped Egg
Seafood Crepes
Melons with Prosciutto
Cornish Hens in an Oyster Sauce
Baked Apples
Green Cabbage Baked in White Wine
Cauliflower in Lemon Juice
Strawberry Mousse

•

Kohlrabi Cream Soup
Whipped Cream Shrimp Roll in a Lemon Cheese Sauce
Romaine Leaves in a Caviar Caesar
Swordfish in Grand Marnier, Sour Cream, and Lobster
Fresh Broccoli
Carrots in Honey, Lime Juice, Cider, and Soy Sauce
Potatoes in a Brown Wine Sauce
Peach Crepes in Amaretto Sauce

•

Baked Oven Vegetable Soup
Portsmouth Pie
Split Pea and Leek Sherbet
Prime Rib of Beef in Peanut Butter and Mushrooms
Baked Celery in Lemons and White Wine
Tomatoes in Orange Juice
Fresh Brussels Sprouts
Blueberry Mousse

•

Catfish Vichyssoise
Ham Kouffle
Cranberry and Plum Sherbet
Lobster Crepes Sauced in Grand Marnier
Baked Oven Vegetables
Cucumbers Baked in White Wine and Curry
Potatoes of the House
Carrots Roasted in Oranges and Raspberries
Sweet Potato and Amaretto Ripple Frozen Mousse

Index

ilyhgk